1,001 BRIGHT IDEAS TO STRETCH YOUR DOLLARS

1,001 Bright Ideas to Stretch Your Dollars

Pinch Your Pennies
Hoard Your Quarters
Collar Your Dollars

Cynthia Yates

VINE BOOKS

Servant Publications
Ann Arbor, Michigan

Vine Books is an imprint of Servant Publications especially designed to serve evangelical Christians.

Published by Servant Publications
P.O. Box 8617
Ann Arbor, Michigan 48107

Cover design by Multnomah Graphics

95 96 97 98 99 10 9 8 7 6 5 4 3 2 1

Printed in the United States of America
ISBN 0-89283-899-X

Library of Congress Cataloging-in-Publication Data

Yates, Cynthia
1,001 bright ideas to stretch your dollars : pinch your pennies, hoard your quarters, collar your dollars/Cynthia Yates.
p. cm.
Includes index.
ISBN 0-89283-899-X
1. Home economics—Accounting. 2. Budgets, Personal. I. Title. II. Title: One thousand one bright ideas to stretch your dollars. III. Title: One thousand and one bright ideas to stretch your collars.
TX326.Y38 1995
640'.42—dc20 95-3592
CIP

To God Be the Glory.
To Everyone Else,
Thanks.

Acknowledgments

After God, my husband. Joseph, this is my chance to say before the world that I am blessed to be your wife.

Then my son. Joshua, my heart explodes with joy as you faithfully serve the Master.

Everyone else—my cheerleaders: Leslie, Jo, Joyce, Grace and Jim, Joe and Flo. My workforce: my sister Anne, who stayed up past her bedtime. H.E., for his determination and servant's heart. Courtney, for showing up at the right time.

My editors: Beth and Heidi.

My helpers: Rick Andres, Doug Becker, Donna Berglund, Linda Brevik, Kevin Cunningham, Carol Dorsey, Robert Gornick, Kristin Reinhart, Greg Harper, Dean Hoyt, Beth Larson, Dottie Maitland, Carol Newlan, Hank Olson, Phoebe Paterson, Jeff Penrod, Gerald Roff, Gary Stempin, Tedi Svare, Fran Tabor, Dave Thomas, Muffie Thomson, Sam and Shirlene Waldenberg, and Deborah Yarborough, DVM.

And, of course, Grim.

Contents

Please Read This Introduction

When I decided to write a book on frugal living, I thought I knew it all. The book is written, and I am now aware of things I didn't know *at all*. And that is my message: ***There is so much we don't know.***

There is much we don't know about buying food, clothes, and cars, about credit and finance, about carpet, drapes and vacuum cleaners, water, gas and electricity. So much we need to know to cut corners, live frugally, and have money left at the end of each month.

This book shares hints, tips, and advice. It covers generalities—certainly each subject merits a book of its own!

Join me in discovery. Meet my sour friend and sidekick, Grim. Shake your head a little, sigh some, maybe even smile out loud. I guarantee a pleasant journey!

ABOUT ME

Though this book is written for Christian women and published by a Christian firm, I know that many others will read it.

Some may even wonder why I chose to bring "religion" into this. Let me explain:

Simply, I am nothing without my Lord. I could no more separate myself from Him than shed my skin, fly to the moon, or broad-jump the Grand Canyon. I joyfully cling to Jesus. It is by His amazing grace alone that I have managed any of this at all. I have changed from the kind of person I used to be, thanks to the One who provides for us all.

ONE

Ten Commandments for Thrifty Living

I don't want to be a tightwad. I want to be frugal. I want to celebrate life, to surround myself with beauty, to be content, whatever state I am in.

I want to manage my finances, to organize my routine, and to use my possessions wisely. I want to budget resources and time, to help others, and to bring glory to God.

The Thrifty Person's Credo

This is my creed. Over time and through determination I have developed a life of frugal living with flair. It is a happy life packed with activity and surprise, a life honored with chatter and crowded tables. It is a sensitive and caring life that reaches to others with outstretched hands, a life offered in gratitude to the service and glory of my holy God. That is how I live.

If that is how you want to live, I give you my hand in friendship to eagerly share my system; a bit of friendly advice as incentive for you to turn to simpler times, to be a better steward of money and possessions, to share the abundance of God's blessing with people less fortunate.

Unyielding demands force many of us to plan an agenda before our feet hit the floor each day. We are nurses, caregivers, playmates, judges and juries to our children. We cook, bake, and decorate, with enough sizzle left over to dazzle our husbands. Our minds inventory every important birthday and anniversary, every can of tuna or tomato sauce in the cupboard, every shirt that needs ironing, every doctor's appointment or school function, and know when the milk is running low. We wash, dry, and put away. We pet the dog, haul the trash, and save for rainy days. And many of us are eager to get back to basics by applying biblical standards to daily routine.

"Daily routine" is expensive. Children cost money. So do birthdays, doctors, and groceries. Do life's costly demands harangue you and lead to frenzy and exhaustion? Does debt deny you the joy and contentment rightfully yours as a child of the King? Do you earnestly want to jump off the merry-go-round and stop your endless cycle of "gimme-gimme-gotta have"?

DEBT

Financial pressure ranks high on the list of demons that plague everyday life. And when this demon throws you into its slippery-sided pit you often find yourself deeper in the hole when you try to claw out. What you need is a helping hand. You need someone to guide you onto solid ground as you work with gritty determination, foothold by foothold, to reach the top. You need someone who has gone this way before.

I know what it is like. I clawed and fought my way to the top of that pit of debt—and slid right back down, time after time. Each time, I ended deeper in debt than when I started. Impulse buying or the lure of easy credit championed over reason. But I was determined to get out of that pit. And I finally did.

Now, if I am not the "Queen of Frugal Living with Flair," I am at least in the Royal Court! Though my husband and I claim a modest income, we wear quality clothing, our tummies are full, we entertain countless guests each year, and the bill collector stays clear of our door. How do we manage? This book shares our lifestyle, our money-saving secrets, our common-sense approach to daily routine, and our earnest intent to share with others. Through necessity, sensible stewardship, and bull-headed determination I am working toward my master's degree in thrifty living. You can too!

TEN COMMANDMENTS FOR THRIFTY LIVING

Over time, I noticed certain principles that apply to all areas of frugal living. I have dubbed these the *Ten Commandments for Thrifty Living:*

1. ROLL UP YOUR SLEEVES!
2. ORGANIZE YOUR WORLD!
3. USE THINGS UP!
4. WASTE NOT!
5. DISCOVER YOUR CREATIVE GENIUS!
6. LEARN PRICES! LEARN PRICES! LEARN PRICES!
7. PRESENTATION IS EVERYTHING!
8. ADJUST YOUR ATTITUDE!
9. OUT WITH IMPULSE!
10. HONOR GOD!

Let's spend some time with each one.

1. Roll up your sleeves! Working toward a frugal lifestyle and maintaining success is not for those who "low-impact" their way through life. It takes grit and determination and hard work. Let's face it: One reason we succumb to costly groceries is convenience and ease in preparation. It takes effort to cook from scratch! Our lives are busy and stress is high. We crave things that satisfy momentary needs to make life easier. We put off better discipline until "tomorrow," but tomorrow never comes. If you are determined to develop thrifty habits, say hello to tomorrow—today! Take a deep breath, roll up your sleeves, and expect to be busy.

2. Organize your world! Organization is the rock on which we build success. And list-making is the cornerstone of organization. I have become a consummate list-maker. I list items to buy and limit myself to the list. I list stops to make with my car, in the best order for gas savings. I list events, job requirements, calls to make.... Using lists has aided immeasurably in maintaining my balance and proves invaluable in stewardship of time and money.

Organize your space: your refrigerator, freezer, spice rack, cupboard, closet, car trunk, anyplace you have an accumulation of things. Every time I organize my refrigerator I find something that needs eating soon. If my storage areas are organized, I know what I already have, so I buy only what I need.

3. Use things up! Put down this book, walk to your kitchen sink, open the cabinet below and have a look. Go ahead. I'll wait.

What did you find? Probably that you need to organize, right? I bet you found an assortment of old dog collars, light bulbs, bug spray, half-used bottles of every cleaning product to grace supermarket shelves, rusted scrubbing pads (we will talk about those things later), rolls of once-wet paper towels, an old potato, several million bud vases (why do we keep those things, anyway?), grit from dishwashing detergent, and enough empty mayonnaise jars to float a battleship (we will talk about jars later, too!). Use things up! Most of you could clean your house for a year without buying one cleaning product—if you simply started using everything you already have.

The same goes for everything in your home. Yes, it is nice to have spare toilet paper. And it is swell when a sale comes along. There is always going to be a sale on toilet paper! Honest. Keep a spare six-pack and use the rest. (This rule does not apply if you shop by dogsled.)

Think about this for a minute. Your intent is to save money, right? Why do you spend money for things that merely occupy space? Think of the candles in the kitchen drawer, the notecards on the desk, the hair conditioner in the medicine cabinet. Do you randomly walk around and put dollar bills in dresser drawers or on shelves? Of course not! Use things up! You will have fun in the process!

4. Waste not! Never, ever, waste! If you have no need for something find someone who does. Several suggestions in the food chapter pivot around this important principle. Do not allow your children to waste. Teach them now. When you waste you dishonor God and the blessings He gives you. When you waste you steal from the mouths and off the backs of others.

Honestly look at your home environment. Do you see waste? Of food? Of natural resources? Of utilities? Of your gifts? Not only does waste add up to dollars and cents, it adds up to offense against our faithful God.

5. Discover your creative genius! Be creative: Dare to break a few rules. Rules like: *We must have meat and potatoes for dinner! We always do it this way! My husband only eats blahblahblah! My children only eat blahblahblah!*

I don't suggest you whip up oatmeal paste and Jello. I do suggest you use creativity to put some zing into meatless meals or resourceful recreation. Let me tell you what I mean: To this day, our most enjoyable and interesting meals are those I plan around that soon-to-be expired item in the refrigerator. Or an item that's been on the shelf for seven years! On a recent reorganizing foray I found an old jar of gourmet chocolate sauce. I whipped up a batch of sweet dough, rolled it out, sprinkled on nuts, shmeared on the chocolate, jelly-rolled the whole thing and presto! Chocolate mini-rolls!

When some of your genius ends in disaster, laugh and defrost a pizza. Or have cereal for dinner. If your husband complains, stick a meatball in his Corn Flakes.

6. Learn prices! Few rules are more important than this one if you want to save money. Whether it's for a jar of pickles or a VCR, a long-distance phone call or a car, learn prices! Know a good buy. With this rule, practice makes perfect. Start small and learn the regular price and the sale price of items you purchase often.

Never, ever, ever stand idly by without watching your prices rung up on the cash register! If you are overwhelmed with children or a big load of groceries, pick a line that will cause less stress, use a familiar clerk, and ask that prices be entered when you can monitor.

I know clerks get testy. I know you might feel anxious or embarrassed, but you ***can*** do this. If you can't monitor the cash register, check your receipt in the car or at home. This is an important principle. We were once charged $70 for shampoo. It was an easy mistake to catch, but I shudder to think how much money we might donate to stores because of human ***and scanner*** error at the checkout. If you find a mistake, speak up—politely of course.

7. Presentation is everything! This is my favorite principle! Presentation! Presentation is about using pretty things. Having company for dinner? Go bananas! Do the unusual. Make your table rumba! Dig through drawers, look on shelves. Present your food with flair. I heard that 80 percent of a dinner's success depends on presentation. No more pork chop on a plate without pizzazz! Put it on a puddle of applesauce. Serve a super salad! Plop edible flowers on top! Be brave with biscuits! Bake them in a cast iron skillet and serve with pork 'n' beans!

The same goes for you and your home. Have an old shawl? Drape it on the couch. Or wrap it around your shoulders and greet your guests with gusto! You will amaze yourself, I promise, if you keep this simple phrase in the front of your noggin: "Presentation is everything!"

8. Adjust your attitude! We will talk soon about what the Bible says. We will talk about verses in Scripture that warn about the love of money, or that admonish us when we covet. We hear so much about positive attitude—is it okay to have one? Yes! If your focus is on Christ, if your motive is not greed, if your goal is sensible stewardship, a positive attitude is not only biblical, it is a command.

Attitude affects everything we do in life. In this book I talk about celebrating, living with gusto, and being motivated, but I talk that way as one who slithered down into that slippery-sided pit so often I know my way blindfolded. You will have dreary days. We all do. You are not Wonder Woman; you never will be. So just hang up your cape and rest awhile. If you need incentive in the attitude department, pick up your Bible and turn to Psalms. Put on praise music.

Pray without ceasing. And recall a favorite phrase of ours: "Draw a circle around yourself and be content with where you are."

9. **Out with impulse!** I am convinced that the Dow Jones average has something to do with all of us buying those tiny nail clippers on chains at the check-out. Or thin mints that used to be a penny but now cost more than dinner out! Or the latest gossip rag. *Do not do it.* Do not buy on impulse. Use your list when you shop for groceries. Put on blinders when looking for a specific piece of clothing. Be careful. Ask yourself if you really need the item. Drive it around in your cart and think. Chances are you can live without it.

10. **Honor God!** We made a rule in our home long ago: We do not allow any thing, any behavior, any speech, any music, any video, any TV show that would hurt the heart of our holy God or blaspheme His holy name. We try hard to abide by this rule.

The Bible tells us we are to be in the world but not of it. Being in the world is a real challenge. The world is filled with allure—it beckons us to buy happiness, beauty, success, popularity, and contentment. King Solomon said in Ecclesiastes 5:10, "Whoever loves money never has money enough; whoever loves wealth is never satisfied with his income." Never let the love of things or your quest for a certain lifestyle rob you of your first love, the Lord Jesus Christ.

Yet keep something in mind: God is not a grump! He cherishes you and knows your every need. And it was He who ordained feasts and festivals in the Bible!

COMMANDMENT #11

Do not be surprised if you stumble. As a matter of fact, *plan* to relax all of these principles from time to time! (Except #10!) Don't set yourself up for failure. The last thing you need is a dose of guilt because you are not achieving "Maximum Thrift Potential" in the first forty-five minutes! Here is how I look at it: Tired of your diet?

Eat a candy bar and get back on the scale tomorrow. Tired of rigid discipline? Zone out watching a funny video. Need a boost? Spend a little money. After all, you put it away for a rainy day, didn't you?

CHARACTER

What does character have to do with frugal living? Plenty! When we talk of character we mean such things as moral strength, goodness, virtue, honor, and righteousness.

The Bible teaches us about character and counsels us that thriftiness is a virtue indeed. It also counsels us about the pursuit of money: "Do not wear yourself out to get rich; have the wisdom to show restraint. Cast but a glance at riches, and they are gone, for they will surely sprout wings and fly off to the sky like an eagle" (Proverbs 23:4-5).

The Bible says much more. Are you a Christian woman? The Bible says you are worth more than jewels if your character is noble. Let's look at Proverbs 31:

> She sets about her work vigorously; her arms are strong for her tasks. *(Roll up your sleeves!)*
>
> She watches over the affairs of her household and does not eat the bread of idleness. *(Organize!)*
>
> She gets up while it is still dark; she provides food for her family and portions for her servant girls. *(Use things up!)*
>
> She opens her arms to the poor and extends her hands to the needy. *(Waste not!)*
>
> She speaks with wisdom, and faithful instruction is on her tongue. *(Discover your creative genius!)*
>
> She sees that her trading is profitable, and her lamp does not go out at night. *(Learn prices!)*
>
> She makes coverings for her bed; she is clothed in fine linen and purple. *(Presentation!)*
>
> She is clothed with strength and dignity, she can laugh at the days to come. *(Adjust your attitude!)*

She considers a field and buys it; out of her earnings she plants a vineyard. *(Out with Impulse!)*
Charm is deceptive, and beauty is fleeting but a woman who fears the Lord is to be praised. *(Honor God!)*
Her children arise and call her blessed, her husband also, and he praises her. *(Bonus points!!)*

A word of caution: The apostle Paul warned Timothy that the love of money is a root of many evils. That verse could never apply to me! Or so I thought. I regarded those as words for people who had money but wanted more, for the skinflint who hoarded his loot, or for the person obsessed with making the first million. Nope, clearly no application to my life!

Then one day the Lord brought me up short. I had groused for weeks about a sudden change in our property tax assessment. "Woe is me" was my chant. "How will we ever manage? This tax is unfair!..." Until He gently spoke to my spirit and reminded me of a few things. An actual conversation might sound like this: "Daughter, have I not always taken care of you? Why do you mock me so by wringing your hands and whining all over town! Your focus is a little off these days; look back to Me."

Sometimes my worry has become obsession and our money crunch has kept me pinned down, away from His liberating arms. Does that ever happen to you? Ask yourself some questions:

- Does my worry over finances absorb my thoughts?
- Do I consider myself orphaned by God because things are not going as well as I would like financially; have I pulled myself out of His reach?
- What does it say about my trust in the faithfulness and providence of my Father when I complain so bitterly?
- The Bible says, "Thou shalt not covet." Do I covet things, security, financial stability?

We all stand guilty of these sins, don't we? How well He knows our human frailties! That is why He gave us His written Word, to guide us, and His living Word, His Son, to lead us. "Don't worry," Jesus says to us. "Tomorrow will take care of itself" (see Luke 12:22-34). And just as Jesus taught us to pray, "Give us this day our daily bread," so it is that if we ask, seek, and knock it will be given to us within His perfect will.

TWO

Food for Thought

Can you have your cake and eat it, too? I think so. I think you can grind your own coffee beans, have a little gourmet food, buy cold-pressed olive oil, and still save pocketsful on groceries. I have been doing it for years!

My intent is not to make things hard for you, or to make you feel guilty for not enduring a threadbare existence. My purpose is to share hundreds of money-saving strategies and start you on the road to frugal living with flair!

Let's begin with food: We live to eat and eat to live. We can live without a roof, we can live without many clothes, we can live without a car, we can live without furniture, but we cannot make it too far without food. How are you budgeting your food dollars? From what I see in some of your shopping carts, not too well. Would you like to save money at the grocery store? This chapter is dedicated to you!

A FAMILY AFFAIR

It happened time and again. My husband Joe usually sounded the alarm, calling our son Josh into urgent conference. "Mom is on a kick again, batten down the hatches!" And oh, how right he was! I've been on health-food kicks, no-red-meat kicks, no-milk kicks, raw-food kicks, on and on to the point of humor.

My small family rarely raised a hand in protest. They patiently lived through carrot meatloaf with the flavor of Styrofoam, deer-and-refried-bean "hamburger" with the texture of a Berber rug, and vegetable stroganoff that looked and tasted like dog food.

You may not be as fortunate. Some of you have mighty finicky eaters in your home: forty-five-pound munchkins who would no more eat a carrot than sprout wings.

How do you get the kids to go along with thrifty changes in the food department? How do you get children to skip the boxed cereal aisle without throwing a fit? Ownership.

Give your children ownership. Sit them down and tell them why you are intent on saving money, how you think this can be accomplished, and ask them to make suggestions. Ask them to specifically make suggestions about food. Use coins to demonstrate the difference in cost between Sugarfrosted-superfluffyOs and pancakes or oatmeal. Do this ***after*** a dynamite breakfast of pancakes shaped like Mickey Mouse or oatmeal with a choice of colorful toppings. Roll up your sleeves and be creative!

And turn to the Bible. Spend time in preparation for this encounter and mark verses you would like your children to read, like: "Better a dry crust with peace and quiet than a house full of feasting, with strife" (Prv 17:1). Ask them what God says about being a good steward. Ask them what you could do with the savings. For instance, how can the money you save by developing a thrifty lifestyle be used to help others?

Don't be too rigid. I believe it is important to allow each family member a luxury. Let each person choose a "can't-live-without" food. If it is something you cannot buy on a regular basis, keep that item as a special gift idea. When your child has touched your heart or accomplished something, or when you just want to show your deep love, why not wrap a special box of Fluffy-Os with a pretty ribbon? You can do it, Mom. And have fun to boot!

This chapter is divided into four categories: food purchase, food storage, food preparation, and recipes. Many suggestions are timeless, many are already in practice in your home. I hope I add to your arsenal by sharing hints on one of my favorite subjects.

FOOD PURCHASE

She rises while it is yet night to provide food for her household.

Proverbs 31:15, RSV

This is where it all starts, where the rutabaga meets the road, so to speak. But not all roads lead to the same place....

The mighty supermarket. This is probably where you shop most. You pull up, grab a cart, hoist a kid in the seat and off you go. Drudgery or adventure? Calamity or challenge? Want some helpful information? Meet your grocer. I did. His name is Doug. And this is what Doug told me:

Most supermarkets expect a profit of 2 percent on goods. There are, however, "price-sensitive" products that, when sold, cause the store to lose some or all of that profit margin. Sometimes, a store may even *lose* money on some items due to price wars caused by competition between markets and consumer demand. Price-sensitive items commonly include mayonnaise, baby food, sugar, and tomato or cream of mushroom soup.

Vendors compete with each other when selling their line of food to supermarkets. That is one reason for seasonal price fluctuations. A list of seasonal sales comes later in this section.

"Ad money" is given to stores by food manufacturers. Some markets use the ad money to offset losses by lowering prices overall. These establishments will often have "in-house" sales, but do not publish weekly flyers for newspapers.

Grocer Doug's most important tips for you are:

1. *Find a market you can trust.* He told me that the people who operate markets know their customers are demanding higher levels of service. This is what I suggest:

Find a market that offers attentive service and quality control in all departments. A store that advertises everyday low prices and in-store specials is a good choice. Also look for a store that accepts all competitor's coupons. It is not usually smart to drive around town for sales.

2. *Study grocery store ads.* This will help you learn prices and guide you in store selection. Many markets offer sales on a few products but are higher priced on non-sale items. Find a store offering consistently lower prices and you will benefit overall.

Health food stores. Even though we keep the sugar bowl full, I tend toward the natural. I buy in bulk at my favorite health food store. Bulk-buying is sensible for us because I can buy as *little* as I need, and am not paying packaging costs.

If you decide to shop in a health food store, I recommend that you start slowly. My first ventures left me perplexed: For months I bought strange things, toted them home, put them in jars—and later threw them away. Buying from this kind of store takes skill and savvy developed over time. But if you are intent on saving money, this is an excellent place to begin.

3. *What to buy.* Herbs, spices, beans, grains, cereals, flour, powdered milk, rice, raisins, and nuts are usually less expensive when bought in bulk. I am fortunate to shop at a store that has an active trade and steady product turnover, which is an important feature. I buy organic produce when I can. Organic, however, is often more expensive. I believe that the money I save on other grocery items compensates for this luxury.
4. *Words of caution:* Stay away from anything prepackaged and from the supplement aisle. Savings on bulk beans will become laughable if you get pulled in by vitamin claims. If you buy vitamins, know your prices!

It is unrealistic to expect every store to post a statement of Christian faith on the door, but I caution you to consider where you spend your money. As a Christian apologist I am well-informed about New Age and Eastern religions. Some health food stores are deeply steeped in practices and philosophies which are regarded as dangerous to the spiritual well-being of Christians. Should you spend your money in such a store? The choice, of course, is yours. Food itself will not harm you spiritually.

Wholesale warehouse store. This kind of store is popping up all over the country. Does it make sense to shop in a warehouse? Most certainly—*if you know your prices!* Supermarkets regularly feature "loss leaders" that compete with or beat wholesale prices.

I shop in a warehouse store for specific items. I have brought home stupendous buys, often on products other than food. I can buy large quantities of staples such as pasta, sugar, and coffee at good savings. The warehouse store closest to us, however, is miles from home. Our infrequent trips to this place require thought and planning.

A warehouse store, if handy, is ideal for a large family that can benefit from volume purchases. It is not sensible to buy volumes of an item that is not a fast mover in your home. This is no ordinary supermarket! The price per item may be much less, but you usually must buy large quantities.

Also consider warehouse membership fees: will you purchase enough to warrant the dues? Our yearly fee is thirty dollars. Bear in mind that the fee is quickly absorbed when buying large-ticket non-food products such as a TV or stereo.

Outlet stores. I can buy bags of more-than-day-old bakery products at a nearby outlet for a dollar or two. If you have a pile of friends coming to picnic, this is a good deal. (Especially if they are young adults who forage to exhaustion in your refrigerator.)

Ready for some friendly advice on how to save money buying food?...

$uper $avers

5. *Shop with a list.* Stick to the list.
6. *Buy only what your family will eat.* Why buy bell peppers on sale if they give your husband heartburn, or bananas when your children eat oranges? Buying something that will go to waste is not very frugal at all.
7. *Do not shop when you are hungry*—especially if your store has free samples. They will taste so good you will have to buy some!
8. *Leave the kids at home when possible.*
9. *Eye-level products are often more expensive.* Did you know that? True.
10. *Never buy groceries from a vendor who drives to your door.* Compare those prices!
11. *Buy seasonally!* Ever wonder why grapes suddenly plummet in price? Grape harvest. Or why bananas are cheaper in summer? Summer vacation (bananas are a staple in the lunch box). Ever wonder why granulated, powdered, and brown sugar prices slump around Thanksgiving? Competition!

Certain times of year present good bargain opportunities to the consumer. Holiday demands cause vendors to compete with each other for your grocer's attention; growing seasons bring us bountiful crops and abundant supply; and economic factors affect us all.

Develop the habit of buying seasonally. Relish the idea of biting into fresh strawberries when summer is peeking over spring's shoulder. Enjoy biting into a good steak on a dreary January night. Stock up on staples when merchants lower prices on baking supplies.

I plan several south-of-the-border meals for spring to celebrate the fifth of May (Cinco de Mayo). In summer, I present platters of sliced radish, cucumber, and tomato with a chunk of bread. I serve apple cobbler in autumn.

12. *Buy smaller if it's better,* as in eggplant and other produce. Bigger fruits and vegies can be tougher, grainier, and even bitter. By the way, buy eggplant that seems heavy for its size.

Seasonal Sales - Groceries

March - corned beef and cabbage
April/May - Mexican food products
June/July - pop, beer, potato chips, charcoal, paper plates, marshmallows, ketchup
November/December - turkey, pumpkin, canned milk, powdered and brown sugar, cranberries, chocolate chips, walnuts, cream cheese, baking ingredients

Seasonal Sales - Produce

January - citrus fruits
February - South American grapes, citrus fruits
March - South American grapes, citrus fruits, cabbage
April - asparagus, artichokes
May - asparagus, strawberries
June - stone fruit, local onions, strawberries
July - melon, California grapes, strawberries, corn, iceberg lettuce, bell pepper
August - best time for July items, cucumbers
September - apples (new crop), pears, corn, squash
October - apples (best time), squash, potatoes, yams
November - citrus season starts
December - citrus fruits, bananas (for baking), onions

13. *Psst… want to know a little-known secret?* Most stores will break up bunches of produce to sell you a smaller amount. It's true! Don't make a pest of yourself, but if you need a little bit of something, like cauliflower or cabbage, just ask. I buy celery this way. (Be sure it will be the same price per pound.)

14. *Coupon fever!* Once upon a time, I was talking to my counterpart, the ever-pessimistic Grim. We were discussing the meaning of life. Naturally, the subject of money-saving coupons came up. Ever the skeptic, Grim wagged his tongue and proclaimed that all coupon-users are aardvarks.

    "May I have a quarter?" I asked politely. "Certainly," said my dour friend, who reached into his pocket for the coin. "Why, thank you," I said quite properly. I then proceeded to walk to the door, fling it open, and throw the quarter as far as I could. I smiled and strode into the next room, leaving Grim standing at the door, which was still open, as was his mouth.

15. *Only use a coupon for something you ordinarily buy.*

16. *Use your coupon when the item is also on sale.* Double-whammy. Stores sometimes offer coupons a week or so before a product is put on sale. If you can wait, hold the coupon awhile to see if sale prices are posted.

17. *Always bring your coupons when you shop.* Browse through your stash occasionally to jog your memory and to discard expired coupons.

18. *Organize your coupons.* My friend Leslie has a small suitcase in which to store her coupons! I have an old wallet that works fine, dividing the coupons into categories: dairy, baby, drinks, paper products, meat, snacks, cereal, baking, pets, canned goods, hygiene, miscellaneous.

19. *Bulletin boards or coupon bins* can sometimes be found in stores. There you will find additional coupons or rebate offers.

20. *Put an asterisk (*) next to each coupon item on your grocery list* so you do not forget—and always write the ad cost next to the item.

21. *Shop ads!* There may be a time when it is worthwhile to shop more than one store; for instance, if another store is advertising a product that is a sensational buy. These are called "loss leaders." These can also be gimmicks, with small print qualifying or limiting your purchase. Use common sense. Is it sensible for you to trek to the other store? It might be. (See chapter 14 for driving

cost.) If you decide to shop the store with the ad, buy the ad product *only*.

22. *Buy sales!* Another way of stating this is "Try not to buy retail." This is not always possible, but if you know your prices you will develop savvy and this principle will become second nature.

    The commandment on using things up comes into play here. Once you become accustomed to using what you have you will build meals around your freezer, your refrigerator, and your cupboards, rather than around specific menus that require retail-priced ingredients. I usually plan meals a day in advance so I can defrost what I will need. I know my cookbooks well and skim the index to find recipes to match ingredients on hand. Daily routine is built around my creativity. I do buy products at full retail, but not if I can help it!

23. *Do not overbuy!!* Even if something is on sale. What is the sense of buying ten cans of tomato paste when you use, on the average, three a year? Or a ponderous sack of potatoes that will grow into bushes in your basement? It is good sense to have spares on hand, but unless you are concerned about natural or political disaster, it is senseless hoarding to keep huge amounts of extra food.

24. *Check per-ounce price* when comparing item prices.

25. *Bulk buy*—if the bulk cost per ounce represents savings. Always consider your time and the cost of repackaging at home.

26. *If you buy in bulk, be certain to label your purchase* in the store and when you get home.

27. *Spice up your life!* Never, ever, buy spices or herbs in a supermarket unless you can't buy in bulk from health food or bulk stores. Buy small quantities because over time spices lose their strength. Keep in jars away from heat. And label!

28. *Stay clear of processed food.* This includes preseasoned chicken, stuffed pork chops, coleslaw mix, pineapple trimmed and sliced, and even cut-up chicken. Consider the price against the "au naturel" cost. There will be times when you throw this suggestion to the wind, and that's okay.

29. *Stay away from packaged cereals* unless you get a really good sale, can get by with generic, or can judiciously use coupons. I know how hard this may be if you have children. Mute the commercials!

30. *Kids stuck on boxed cereal?* Here's a strategy: Scout up colorful, pourable-type containers for each family member. Encourage the children to decorate and label their own containers. Buy bulk or generic cereal and pour into containers.

    Why, oh, why, do you ask? Read on for a sampling of prices:

Flakes of corn:	brand name—16¢/ounce generic—6¢/ounce
Honey oat things:	brand name—23¢/ounce generic—10¢/ounce
Sweet puffy wheat:	brand name—13¢/ounce generic—7¢/ounce

31. *Do not buy vegetables in little bags with cheese sauce.* They are probably loaded with salt and fat anyway. Make your own sauce. Get creative with seasoning!

32. *Never buy juice in cans or bottles, especially individual servings!* If your children carry a lunch, go back to the old-fashioned thermos. Use frozen or concentrate if buying juice. I read that you can refill an eight-ounce glass of water up to fifteen thousand times for the same cost as a six-pack of pop!

33. *Buy generic products or the store brand.* I know you have heard this before, but it is true: In most cases you will get the same quality.

34. *Buy industrial-sized cans of certain foods.* Can you freeze some of the product in smaller containers? Will the product last long enough in the refrigerator for you to use it all?

35. *Check a sale item against the generic or store brand* before you put it in your cart. Be especially careful of those end-of-the-aisle sale items in supermarkets.

36. *Stock up on meat when it's on sale, if you have a freezer.*
37. *Think twice before buying a side of beef!* My butcher, Rick, says the price we pay per pound is for "hanging weight." Depending on the animal, he estimates around a 52/48 split once the meat is trimmed and prepared. That's 52 percent to you, 48 percent to the trash can.
38. *Buy meat seasonally.* Meat is different from other grocery items. Demand brings prices up. Better cuts of beef, for example, cost more during barbecue season than during winter months.
39. *Veal is expensive.* Period.
40. *Try "family packs" of meat.* You can save money this way, but be ready to roll up your sleeves when you get home, and be certain you have packaging material. Remember to label! Our dogs know there's a goodie in store for them when I come home with family packs. One caution: Don't trip over dogs in your kitchen.
41. *For the chuckwagon...* Have you ever seen a picture of a cow with those puzzle-like lines drawn to divide the animal into parts? One of those lines between the rib and chuck marks something called rib eye on one side and eye of chuck or first-cut chuck on the other side. Same muscle group. But guess which side sells for half the price? So when old Chuck is on sale, go buy some. I do. I tote the meat home, cut out lovely steaks, trim the meat on both sides of the bone to use for stew or stir-fry, and boil the bones to make broth.
42. *Try not to buy lunchmeat at the deli!* Buy a precooked ham or turkey ham and ask the meat department to slice it to your liking. If you make lunches, this is a less expensive way to go. Be certain there is no extra cost involved for slicing.
43. *Consider bone-in shank ham* as a less expensive alternative to boneless, IF you will use the bone. We use the bones for bean soup and then give them to the dogs.
44. *Factor in the weight of bones* when you are buying meat. It may be cheaper to go boneless.

45. *Regard all meat as expensive.* Be careful when ads promote cheap meat. Sometimes, that is exactly what it is! I once bought something called a "chub"—five pounds of ground beef. It was so inexpensive I felt victorious! But it was disgusting. When I formed the meat into hamburgers for the freezer my hands were thick with grease. Once cooked, the meat not only shriveled to nothing, it left a greasy film in our mouths. I didn't even give this to the dogs. Some bargain! When I buy ground beef now, I get a low fat count.

46. *Try chicken thighs as a tasty alternative to boneless breasts.* I bone-out the thighs, cook up the bones and gristle to make stock, feed the gristle to the cats, put the meat between a couple pieces of wax paper and give it a whack with my rolling pin to flatten it.

47. *Tenderize the less expensive cuts.* Have the butcher run them through a tenderizer.

48. *Use marinades.* Rick says less expensive cuts do well with marinade: Delmonico, tri-tip roast, cross rib steak, round steak.

    Do you know why we marinate? Not just for flavor. Remember the cow with the jigsaw puzzle on its back? Better cuts of meat are from the top of the animal. They are prepared by roasting and broiling, with a tender result. Cuts of meat from the legs, belly, and neck have muscle and connective tissue that needs to be broken down. Marinades do this.

    A great way to marinate is in zip-top bags. Or marinate in a glass container and turn with wooden utensils. Unless a recipe calls for a short time, longer marinating yields a better result. So says Rick. And I believe anyone who walks around with a butcher knife!

49. *Never, EVER, buy a dairy product without checking the expiration date!* I pick the package with the longest shelf life, usually found toward the back of the display.

50. *Shredded or sliced cheese costs more.* Ask the meat department if they will slice the brick of cheese you bought on sale. Mine will.

51. *Try freezing sticks of sale-priced butter or margarine.*

Marinade recipes for cheap cuts of beef

- 1/4 c. oil, 1/4 c. wine vinegar, 1/4 c. soy sauce, 1/4 c. chopped onion, 1 tsp. garlic salt, 1 tsp. basil, 1 tsp. salt, 1 tsp. pepper, 1/2 tsp. ginger
- (Children Pleaser!) 1-1/2 c. tomato juice, 1/2 c. chopped onion, 2 Tbs. wine vinegar, 1 clove minced garlic, 1 tsp. salt, 1/2 tsp. hot pepper sauce
- 1/2 c. strong coffee, 1/2 c. soy sauce, 1 Tbs. Worcestershire sauce, 1 Tbs. vinegar, 1 large onion, chopped

Marinade recipes for chicken or beef

- 1/2 c. soy sauce, 1/4 c. honey, 1/2 tsp. garlic powder
- 1/4 c. Worcestershire sauce, 1 Tbs. minced onion, 2 Tbs. lemon juice, 2 Tbs. oil, 1 tsp. salt, 1/2 tsp. minced garlic

52. *Do not buy yogurt in individual containers* unless you have first checked that the price-per-ounce cost is cheaper or unless you need only a little. Buy the quart size. Best bet: Buy plain and flavor it yourself. (See yogurt section later in this chapter.)
53. *Buy cheaper ice cream.* The cheaper the ice cream, the lower the fat. Therefore buying cheap ice cream is not only thrifty, it is good for you! However, I think this is a good place for Commandment #11 to kick in once in a while. (I'll have a double-dip and make mine Rocky Road!)

FOOD STORAGE

He who gathers crops in summer is a wise son, but he who sleeps during harvest is a disgraceful son. **Proverbs 10:5**

What does storage have to do with spending money? Everything! Why be judicious in spending money if you lose your savings through neglect, rot, or decay? Proper storage of food is a critical aspect of thrifty living.

But are you hoarding or storing? Has hoarding food become a hobby? Are you collecting groceries or are you intelligently using and rotating your supply?

I have a one-drawer kitchen. I have no cabinets with doors. My pantry is a shower-sized indentation in our kitchen wall that is lined with wooden shelves. I love my pantry! Colorful tins hold oatmeal, lentils, popcorn, and tea; jars are filled with beans, pasta, cookies, sugar, crackers, and mixes. It keeps me happy and organized at a glance.

Besides common-sense measures regarding such things as refrigeration and sanitation, we should consider three basic methods of storing food: canning, dehydrating, and freezing.

Canning. Much of the food I can has come free of charge from a friend who gardens. How can I go wrong? I enjoy the colorful display in my cupboard, and I appreciate the thrift and nutritional value of canning. Besides, I am never without a hostess gift.

Is it worth it? Canning equipment costs money. You must also consider the time spent preparing food, and the electricity or gas that keeps your canner hot for hours. I own a hot-water bath canner. I borrow a pressure canner. I have accumulated a large number of jars and rings, but I need to buy new lids each year.

If you have storage room, if you will use what you have canned in place of store purchases, if you will continue to can year after year, go ahead and make the equipment investment. Check garage sales and thrift stores first. And do not buy anything damaged; your family's health is serious business.

Dehydrating. My husband's mother gave me a dehydrator. I use it non-stop during harvest season. I dehydrate Italian plums to make prunes, and dry apple rings by the hundreds. Nothing is wasted! I even turn juice and sludge into delicious fruit leather. I do not bother to dehydrate carrots, potatoes, or onions because I purchase them at good prices year round.

If you have a dehydrator, put it to use. My Polish grandmother dehydrated in the oven and in the sun, but without practice these methods may end in waste. Borrow a book from the library about how to use a dehydrator. When foods your family likes are in season or on sale, dry away!

It is common to find a dehydrator in a thrift store after someone's good intention sort of... dried up.

Freezing. I freeze just about everything: leftovers, homemade stock, meat from a great sale, fish from a fisher friend. Among other things, I keep extra coffee beans in the freezer, well-wrapped paint brushes if I am in the midst of a painting job, and a sack of peas as a cold pack for medical emergencies.

54. *If you freeze, wrap food properly* to keep out air, and label, label, label, including date! One day I grabbed a small unlabeled container that I thought was pineapple juice. Into the blender with milk it went. Whirr! A foamy delight! Ick. I had made a milkshake from fish stock. The cats thought it was terrific.

Remember to use things up! After you have had to throw freezer-burned food away, you learn this principle. Fast.

Basic storage supplies. Have on hand a sensible supply of jars (I use old-fashioned jars I've found in thrift stores), tins, labels, food storage bags, freezer bags and paper, markers, masking tape, and clothespins. Clothespins?! Yes! Once you use them in place of "twist ties" to close plastic storage bags, you will wonder how you lived without them.

Produce. If you get to know anyone in your supermarket, get to know your produce manager. My green-grocer's name is Kevin. I often saunter into the mega-market store where I shop and ask someone in the produce section, "What's the freshest and most economical buy in your department today?" With the attention given a visiting dignitary, I am guided to all the freshest fruits and vegetables.

Hardly any of us had training in produce care. We have learned by trial and error, learned from our mothers, or not really learned at all. Rot in the vegie bin is not frugal!

Kevin explained that all produce requires proper care for safe and sensible keeping as well as for freshness and vitality. And he told me about the Produce Life Support System (I kid you not). He said that once produce is picked from its source, it begins gradual deterioration. Each item requires proper storage conditions to prolong its useful life.

All produce breathes in carbon dioxide and breathes out oxygen and a gas called ethylene. Six elements are involved in proper produce care:

Respiration. This is important: The faster the produce breathes, the faster it ripens, and the shorter the shelf life. Fast breathers must be slowed down to ensure quality. Strawberries, for instance, breathe ten times faster at 70°F than at 33°F.

Temperature. Fast breathers are stored in cold temperatures to make them slow down. Excessive chilling, however, is counterproductive, causing starches to convert to sugars, which leads to decay. Avocados, for instance, turn black inside when kept at lower than 45°F.

Water. Did you know that most plants are 90-95 percent water? No wonder we eat them when dieting! We have vegetable crispers in our refrigerators to help conserve water. Some vegetables, such as asparagus, are no different from cut flowers in their need for water. Droopy produce is not always too old to use! Many times it can be refreshed in a bath of warm water. Soak in lukewarm water for ten minutes, dry, then put in the fridge for a while. Presto!

Air circulation. This is critical because plants must continue breathing. If too much ethylene accumulates, you have decay. Remove tight-fitting covers or wrappers and replace with loose bags when you store. Carrots must be stored in bags with holes because carrots emit a gas that causes a bitter taste.

Light. Light stimulates photosynthesis, which is why potatoes should be covered. They turn green if stored in excessive light.

Odor control. Produce quickly absorbs the air around it, so off-flavors will develop when bad odors are present. Put a strawberry next to an onion and you are going to have mighty strange-tasting shortcake! Mushrooms are magnets to just about any odor in the area.

Produce Respiration Table

Extremely High: berries, lima beans, avocados, mushrooms, corn, asparagus, peas, broccoli, spinach

Very High: green beans, artichokes, brussels sprouts

Moderate: apricots, bananas, cherries, peaches, nectarines, celery, plums, figs, new potatoes, tomatoes, peppers, carrots, cabbage

Slow: apples, citrus fruits, grapes, kiwi, garlic, onions, mature potatoes, sweet potatoes

Very Slow: nuts, dates, dried fruits

$uper $avers

55. *Keep your supplies organized* so you can tell at a glance if you are running low.
56. *Plastic bags are indispensable* for storing certain produce. But plastic bags accumulate moisture. Some moisture is good and helpful to maintain the item. Too much is not good. Whenever

I use produce I turn the bag inside-out before I return the unused portion to the fridge. I also poke a few "breather" holes in the bag.

57. *Put folded newspaper on the bottom of your crisper.*
58. *Green goop alert!* How many times have you found a sloppy mess in your vegetable crisper when you reached for the radishes? Next time you buy some, whack off the greens, clean the radishes, and store them in a plastic-lidded tub with a folded-up piece of paper towel on the bottom.
59. *Do NOT store potatoes in the refrigerator.* Potatoes should be stored in a dark, dry place. Cold temperatures convert potato starch to sugar which makes black blotches inside your spuds. Also, do not store potatoes with onions, since each gives off gas that affects the other.
60. *Bananas, stone fruit, and tomatoes* should be stored at room temperature unless they are fully mature, when they can be refrigerated (except bananas, which turn black when refrigerated).
61. *Keep plastic produce bags from the grocery store.* Double up and use them as "suitcases" for freezer-wrapped goods. Also use produce bags to store home-baked goods.
62. *Save zip-top bags* unless they have food residue. I dry and reuse the same storage and freezer bags for months!
63. *Use or freeze leftovers promptly.* Kristin makes her own fast food by freezing individual leftovers in meal form. She freezes in microwaveable containers. Remember to label!
64. *Don't keep meat in the freezer too long.* Meat will begin to lose nutritional value after six months in the freezer.
65. *Freeze pieces of meat individually* when processing family packs. Once the meat is frozen solid, store the pieces in larger storage containers. No more contending with those giant hunks of welded-together meat parts that look like modern sculpture.
66. *Pre-freeze berries on cookie sheets.* Again, once frozen, put in a

plastic bag. This keeps them from freezing together.

67. *Use up those to-go coffee cups.* I don't like Styrofoam, but I save every cup that comes my way; they are excellent temporary freezer containers. I freeze just about anything in these small cups. And I can write on them with magic marker—an important feature if you are not fond of fishy milkshakes.
68. *Mark dates on cans,* suggests friend Jim. This is a good idea since canned goods have a shelf life.
69. *Remember the old-fashioned breadbox?* Did you know that bread stales quickly at cold temperatures? Unless you live in a humid place, keep your bread at room temperature in a plastic sack or breadbox.
70. *Getting long on eggs?* Mark the oldest ones with an "X" and use them first.
71. *Ever have leftover frosting?* If it's enough to use on cupcakes or as middle frosting for a cake, freeze it in a container. If it's not enough, freeze it in a small, sturdy plastic bag. When you need frosting for decorating, defrost, add the tiniest bit of water to bring to decorating consistency, mush around in the bag, push all toward a corner, snip a tiny opening, and presto! Instant decorator bag!

FOOD PREPARATION

Lazy hands make a man poor, but diligent hands bring wealth.

Proverbs 10:4

Now we know how to *buy* food and save money and how to *store* food and save money. Let's talk about how you *prepare* food. And let's start with some other cooking methods besides using your kitchen stove....

Microwave. A microwave is significantly less expensive to operate than a stove. My microwave is a workhorse, performing such duties as warming leftovers, melting butter, reheating coffee, cooking vegetables to crispy perfection, and even making iced tea.

72. ***Stay clear of items merchandised with your microwave in mind,*** such as cake mixes, frozen meals, or, especially, ***popcorn.*** Do not yield to the lure of microwave packets. Good quality plain popcorn is remarkably inexpensive and easy to prepare. Use a secondhand electric popper or just a big pot with a lid. Keep your unpopped corn in the freezer to maintain the moisture level necessary for good performance.

Pressure cookers. My sister Sheila gave me an old pressure cooker. Pressure cookers cut preparation time drastically. They are energy efficient, and they retain most of the food's nutrients. Soups and stews are ready in minutes. Want swift and succulent meals from vegetables, whole grains, briskets, and pot roasts? Put some pressure in your cooking.

Don't be intimidated by the contraption as I first was. Mine terrified me at first. I crouched behind a three-foot wooden partition in our kitchen and peeked at the bomb doing a jig on our stove. I crawled on my stomach to a phone, dialed the 800 operator, and called Cook-O-Matic in alarm. "My pressure cooker is going to explode!" I hissed. "Turn it off," hissed back the expert. "I'm too scared to go near it!" I whimpered. The lady sent me a complimentary booklet on pressure-cooker protocol.

You ***might*** find a pressure cooker at a thrift store. Best bet: garage sales. Be careful the rubber gasket is not worn and that openings are not clogged.

Crockpots. Whatever happened to our mighty crockpots? Why did we relegate them to that high kitchen shelf to collect dead spiders and dust? Bring them back! Is there anything finer than the aroma of dinner when you come home at night? All because you took time to throw ingredients in your crockpot in the morning.

73. ***Turkey dinner.*** My all-time favorite is a turkey leg that has been simmering with carrots and onions all day. Turkey legs are

cheap! Ask your butcher to saw off the bony end so you can fit it in your slow cooker. Put it in the pot with pepper, paprika, garlic powder, a bit of water, chunks of carrot, slices of onion. Serve turkey chunks on a fat slice of bread. Or eat caveman style!

Bread machines. I received a bread machine from a relative one Christmas, and I have since baked hundreds of loaves. Besides serving homemade bread to my family, I give it to starving students, use it as hostess gifts, and barter loaves in exchange for fresh fish from fisherman neighbors. Important benefits of the machine are my control of ingredients and the chance to experiment.

Is a bread machine for you? They are expensive. Sit down with paper and pencil to figure it out. You may already buy your bread at a reduced price from an outlet, which makes it more economical. Good bread is not cheap at retail prices. Home-baked bread is not cheap, either.

Even without investing in a machine, it takes time, ambition, and money to make healthful bread. If your family likes bread and if you worry about ingredients, you can justify the cost of good bread by being frugal in other areas.

Homemade or store-bought? Even if you want to save money, to be a good steward, and have a simpler lifestyle, it is unrealistic to expect you to eliminate all convenience from life. There are times when a product or machine clears time for more important purposes.

74. *Homemade is not always thrifty.* On the other hand, simple homemade substitutes can save money. Although I prefer homemade, I find cheaply priced cake or brownie mixes in sale bins. I also benefit from coupon savings. I always have boxed cake mix for an emergency birthday cake, etc. Ever had a guest casually announce, "Today is my birthday"? I have.

My hobby is preparing new recipes. This can challenge my thrifty bone when I need to find unusual ingredients or a way to obtain small quantities. Heavy cream is one such thing: I'm stuck with a pint when I only need a quarter cup. That is not very thrifty! So I substitute when I can. I put my creativity in gear and figure how to prepare recipes by eliminating or substituting an ingredient. Here are some suggestions:

Substitutions

- Bread crumbs - Grind up crackers of any kind.
- Baking chocolate - 3 Tbs. cocoa (I buy it in bulk) to 1 Tbs. oil
- Heavy cream - 3/4 c. milk, 1/3 c. butter
- Light cream - 3/4 c. milk, 3 Tbs. butter
- Cake flour - Use regular flour, reduce each cup by two tablespoons, stir with a whisk to loosen.
- Cornstarch - 1 Tbs. cornstarch = 2 Tbs. flour or 1-1/2 Tbs. instant tapioca.
- Melted shortening - Same amount of salad oil
- Buttermilk - Add 1 Tbs. vinegar or lemon juice to one cup milk.
- Corn syrup - 1/4 c. water and 1 c. sugar
- Rum - Use any available juice or flavor extract.
- Juice - Equal amount of water with 1 tsp. flavoring
- Lemon juice - Use 1/2 tsp. plain vinegar for every tsp. lemon juice. Or freeze lemon slices—no bottles, no rotting, leftover lemons.
- Brown sugar - Add 2 Tbs. molasses to 1 c. granulated sugar, mix well.
- Maple syrup - Buy maple flavoring. The recipe is on the box.

$uper $avers

75. *Read recipes ahead of time.* Twice. Then think them through. Have you ever had company ringing your doorbell just as you discovered dessert must sit in the freezer for 24 hours? Or that you need an ingredient like armadillo meat or yam-flavored banana chips? An emergency trip to the store for dinner or dessert is not economical.

76. *Measure*—unless you are a grandmother. And use a scale.

77. *Use meat as an ingredient, not as the main event.*

78. *Steakout.* Ever provided a big steak for each guest at a cookout? You splurged to begin with, only to watch the cocker spaniel and Labrador retriever devour the leftovers on each plate. Our friend Bukke's rule: Buy half as many steaks as you have guests, cook them (steaks, not guests), cut each steak into three pieces, plop them on a platter, and you enjoy leftovers at midnight. Guaranteed. Give the dogs a bone.

79. *Too much salt in your soup?* Add a couple of slices of raw potato and simmer awhile. Too much pepper? Add butter. Too sweet? Add salt.

80. *Always have powdered milk and powdered buttermilk on hand.* This precludes buying fresh (and more than you need) for recipes. I buy mine in small bulk at our health food store. And whenever you use buttermilk in baking add a pinch of baking soda to counter the acid.

81. *Fruit snacks.* I keep a few pieces of fresh fruit in a basket on the top shelf of my refrigerator, closest to eye level.... It works. We are more inclined to grab an apple or pear right in front of us than to dig around the bottom of the fridge.

82. *Live off your stored goods.* I pledge to live off my refrigerator, freezer and cupboard for certain periods without buying anything unless necessary, sales or not! Try it. Start with a week, then longer. Using things up gets to be habit, as does creativity.

83. *What if someone gives you a bushel of apples?* Free food! But unless you are the Old Woman in the Shoe you are not going to eat them before they waste or turn grainy. Here's what I do:
    - Refrigerate some for snacking and baking.
    - Applesauce! Peel, core, and cook apples in a non-aluminum pan (because of acid) on medium-low to produce sauce consistency. I rarely add sugar to applesauce. Grace adds a bag of red cinnamon candy to hers. Some people add spice, brown sugar, or honey.
    - Apple rings! This is the top job for my dehydrator, drying tray upon tray of apple rings during harvest. I store them in airtight plastic bags and serve bowls filled with this nutritious snack year round.
    - Apple pie! Peel and slice apples as if for a pie, even sprinkle with sugar and spice, freeze uncooked in pie tins. Once frozen, move the "disks" to freezer bags. Ready for baking on demand!
84. *What would you do with a dead banana?*
    - Freeze for future baking use, right in the peel.
    - Use potato masher to combine with oatmeal.
    - Make banana and peanut-butter sandwiches. Yum!
    - Add to cookie dough, instead of some of the shortening.
    - Make a cake:

      You will need:
      2-3 mashed bananas
      1/2 c. soft butter
      3/4 c. honey
      1 tsp. vanilla
      1/2 tsp. salt
      1 egg
      1-3/4 c. each white and whole wheat flour, mixed
      1/2 tsp. cinnamon
      1 tsp. baking soda
      1/2 c. chopped nuts (optional)

Preheat oven to 350°F and grease a 9" x 9" pan. Mix bananas, butter, honey, vanilla, salt. Stir in egg. Mix dry ingredients and nuts, add to banana mixture. Bake 45 minutes or so.

85. *Broth to spare.* I am a consummate broth maker. I sometimes get free beef bones from my butcher, and never discard chicken bones or spare chicken parts before making pots of broth. Not only do many recipes call for broth, I use mine as cooking water to fortify rice or bean dishes. I am aware of sales on canned broth, yet adamantly stick to homemade for these reasons:

- Using leftover bones from meat maximizes my purchase; nothing goes to waste.
- When using store-bought knuckle bones I treat the dogs after making broth. Bone purchase probably costs the same as a can of broth.
- Most important is my control of ingredients. The sodium content in canned broth is out of sight!
- Beef broth: Any bone will do. Knuckle bones with a bit of meat are best. Wash the bone. Leave some fat for flavor. Add bone and seasoning to a few quarts of water. (I add several cloves of garlic and a cut-up onion.) Bring to a boil, cover, and simmer 4 hours. Put in fridge overnight so fat congeals, skim off fat. Freeze in containers and label.
- Chicken Broth: Backs, necks, wing tips and spare parts are left over when I process whole chickens. Into a big pot of cold water they go! I add a bay leaf, chopped celery, carrot and onion, a little salt, a few peppercorns, and bring to a boil. Cover and simmer 4 hours. Process same as beef broth. Do NOT give chicken bones to the dogs!

86. *Shake it up!* A favorite treat is a milkshake about an hour before bedtime. Besides using frozen berries or fresh fruit, make shakes from frozen juice. Never throw the juice from canned fruit down the drain! Freeze in small, individual containers, larger at the top than the bottom (save to-go coffee cups for this). Pour 6

ounces of skim milk into the blender, plop in frozen fruit juice, and give a whirl. Delightful!

87. *Yogurt.* I bought a yogurt maker at a thrift store. This machine works so hard I could justify buying one new. I always have yogurt on hand, and make mine with skim milk. Buy yogurt cultures at the health food store or create a new batch using part of the old. Caution: Really old, expired yogurt will not work as a culture.

If you buy yogurt, quart containers of plain yogurt cost much less than flavored or individual serving sizes. Some things to do with yogurt:

- Eat plain or flavored. Add crunchy grains, cereals, fruits, nuts, coconut. Try this great recipe: Combine 1 c. of yogurt, 1 Tbs. sugar, a dash of almond extract. Blend well and refrigerate at least 2 hours. Serve on peaches.
- Make a dip. Try combining 1 c. of yogurt with 1 c. of cottage cheese, then mix in a twenty-five cent packet of taco flavoring. Chill well.
- Put yogurt on top of things like cereal, hot or cold.
- Use instead of sour cream.
- Make yogurt cream cheese. This is fun! Line a strainer with cheesecloth, plop in a couple cups of yogurt, tie the top with string, hang over a bowl to drain. After several hours you have cream cheese. The liquid left over is called whey. I use it in baking. If I'm not baking soon, guess who gets it on top of their icky dry food? Yep. The dogs.

88. ***And then there's all those sweet crumbs…*** "Why don't you throw those crumbs away!" said Grim. "You are getting too weird, collecting them!" Throw away crumbs from just-baked cookies and cakes? Never! Collect them in a plastic container and store in the freezer or fridge.

- Use to make bottoms of things, like cheesecakes.
- Use to make tops of things, like streusel.

- Sprinkle on hot cereal. (Presentation!)
- Add to cookie batter, etc.
- Sprinkle on ice cream, cottage cheese, or yogurt.

89. *Grow a kitchen garden.* I found a green, multi-tiered, sprout grower at (where else?) a thrift store. I bought alfalfa seeds at the health food store. My entire investment in this "farm" was around a dollar. I make alfalfa sprouts for salads and sandwiches. I stagger sprout growth cycles by starting seeds every other day, otherwise there is too big a crop… sprouts breathe fast! I use the water from sprout growing for house plants.

    You can also sprout mung beans for oriental recipes. First soak a handful overnight. Line a colander with an old, clean dishtowel and pour in the wet beans. Fold the edges of the towel down over the beans, put the whole thing on a pie tin to catch drips, and keep it three days in a dark, warm place (like a cupboard over your stove). Rinse the whole affair in cool water a couple of times a day. Fresh and crisp!

90. *Brew iced tea.* For a fabulously inexpensive drink, put three tea bags into a two-quart pitcher of water. Microwave on high for ten minutes. Add sugar to taste while hot. Add lemon slices for a treat.

    During winter Joe and I drink a pot of tea after dinner. Leftover tea is poured into a glass and put in the fridge, not down the drain.

91. *Get fancy with cakes.* Put chocolate chips in a sturdy little plastic bag and immerse in hot water. After the chocolate melts, snip off a tiny tip from the corner and drizzle chocolate all over your cake or pastries. Presentation!

92. *Make your own bread crumbs and croutons.* Do not throw away old bread! Toast anything not already hard and dry. Whirl in your blender to make crumbs for recipes.

    And if you never made your own croutons to jazz up a salad or a bowl of soup, puh-leeze give this a try:

You will need:

2 c. bread cubes — Melted butter or olive oil

Your own blend of any kind of spices and herbs

Brush bread with butter or oil. Sprinkle with spices. Bake at 375°F for about 10 minutes until crisp. Store in airtight container.

93. *Make your own salad dressing.* Bottled salad dressing is expensive. Make your own. Here is a recipe for Russian dressing using the hot-dog relish that's been sitting in your fridge:

    You will need:

    1 c. mayonnaise or yogurt, 1/4 c. catsup, 3 Tbs. relish, 1 Tbs. lemon juice, horseradish to taste, and a dash of chili powder. Mix together and refrigerate.

94. *Make garlic bread at the table.* Cut one-inch slices of day-old Italian or French bread. Toast in oven till slightly browned. Put bread in serving basket. Give each person a peeled clove of garlic and have good olive oil on the table. Rub garlic on the bread and drizzle very lightly with the oil. Wow! (Serve breath mints for dessert.)

95. *Try one of Joe's concoctions!* My husband believes in one-pot cooking. Sometimes I am dismayed when he proudly serves dinner. His latest: Cook egg noodles, drain. Add 1 tsp. butter, mix. Add one can of chopped clams, drained. (Buy clams on sale. Freeze clam juice for chowder.) Grate any kind of cheese on top. Serve. Then say, "I'm a good cook, hunh?"

96. *Want instant spaghetti sauce?* Spend a quarter on a packet of spaghetti seasoning. Keep it on hand to mix with a can of tomato sauce or a can of tomatoes.

97. *Meatballs in a hurry.* Get your pan hot, then add a little oil. When hot, add ground meat which has been patted into a one-inch thick rectangle. As it cooks, use an implement to separate the size "meatballs" you want.

98. *To oil or not to oil?* Grim and I argued about this one. When cooking pasta, do not use oil in water if serving with sauce—it won't cling to the pasta as well.

RECIPES

Better a meal of vegetables where there is love than a fattened calf with hatred. **Proverbs 15:17**

My day-to-day cooking is more "method" than recipe, and there are three indispensable ingredients in my "Thrift Hall of Fame": pasta, rice, and beans. These three staples are the foundation upon which I build most meals, variations limited by other ingredients on hand. They are inexpensive, versatile, and healthful! First, some pasta ideas:

99. Sort-of lasagna. Substitute ANY pasta as layers in lasagna.

100. Pasta salad. This is good hot or cold. Cook pasta of your choice. Add peas, water chestnuts, broccoli pieces, tuna—the sky is the limit! Mix with Italian dressing.

101. Dead cheese pie. Kids love this! It uses up that old cheese you have in your refrigerator. Even great in the lunch box.

You will need:
2 c. cooked spaghetti
1-2 Tbs. melted butter or olive oil
2 Tbs. dry parsley
1/2 c. chopped onion
4-6 eggs
about 2 c. old cheese, crumbled or shredded
salt and pepper

Heat butter and olive oil; sauté onions and parsley, let cool a bit. Beat eggs in a bowl and add some of the cheese. Mix everything together and spread into 9" x 9" pan. Bake 25 minutes at 350°F. Cut into squares. This recipe is a keeper!

102. Spaghetti sauce. This is one meal you should always have on hand for emergency company. We always have homemade canned or frozen sauce for just this purpose. I prefer a lighter, low-fat sauce, but this recipe is an artery-clogger—and a show-stopper! (Do not serve this to friends watching fat intake.)

Sauté in a blend of 1/2 c. butter and 1/2 c. oil:
4 medium onions, chopped
5 cloves garlic, chopped
2 Tbs. dry parsley

Add: 12 oz. tomato paste
16 oz. tomato puree*
1/2 c. water
2 Tbs. Worcestershire sauce
dash of hot sauce

Optional: Add 1 pound browned ground meat OR browned hot Italian sausage (our favorite)

Cook all *at least* 1 hour. All day in the crockpot is infinitely better! Trust me.

* *Buy industrial-sized can of puree to save big $$. Freeze unused puree in small batches and use for homemade pizza sauce—or more spaghetti.*

103. *Garlic and oil sauce.* If your family likes the taste of garlic and if you can buy good bulk olive oil, this will drop you in your tracks! It is embarrassingly easy and reduces company to licking fingers and plates.

You will need
1/2-1 c. olive oil
3 cloves finely minced garlic
1/2 tsp. salt
1/2 tsp. pepper
1/4-1/2 c. cooking water from spaghetti

Heat oil in frying pan, add garlic till soft. Add seasoning and water; blend. Cook about a minute; pour over spaghetti.

104. *Noodle Kugel.* Use pasta for dessert! So what if you don't have egg noodles? Use what you have.

You will need
1/2 pound egg noodles
1 Tbs. sugar
2 eggs plus 1 egg white
1/2 tsp. cinnamon
raisins
dash of salt

Boil noodles till done, drain and combine with other ingredients. Pour into greased 8" x 8" baking dish. Bake about an hour at 300°F until lightly browned on top. Cut into squares.

Rice. Unless cooking an oriental dish, I use brown rice. Use whatever kind of rice you wish, but stay away from that instant stuff.

105. *Stir fry.* This is the number-one use-it-up meal in our home. We have an electric wok which (You can say this by heart by now, can't you?) we bought in a thrift store. I heat some oil in a frying pan or the wok, add a bunch of vegetables that have been cut into small pieces, stir steadily until they are crisp-cooked, add a bit of water or soy sauce if it begins to stick, and serve over a big plate of rice.

If you want to add meat, cook thin strips in a separate pan or cook in the wok first and set aside in a warm place until you stir everything back together. If you are ambitious, start a half hour before cooking and marinate meat pieces in a combination of 2 Tbs. soy sauce, 1 tsp. cornstarch, and 2 Tbs. water.

106. *Rice with leftovers.* We make meals of whatever is getting "long-in-the-tooth" in our vegie bin—and rice. This is the ultimate in cheap and satisfying meals.

107. Mexican rice.

You will need:
3 Tbs. butter/oil
2/3 c. chopped onion
1 c. white rice
1 c. chopped green pepper
1 can whole tomatoes, chopped
1 tsp. chili powder
1 tsp. salt

In medium-heavy skillet sauté onion in butter or oil. Stir in rice, pepper, chili powder, tomatoes, and salt. Add 2 c. water. Bring to a boil, reduce heat, cover tightly, and simmer for 20 minutes.

108. Rice and peas. This is an easy and sublime dish.

You will need:
2 Tbs. butter
1/3 c. finely chopped onion
2 Tbs. finely chopped fresh parsley
1 c. white rice
2 c. boiling water
1 c. frozen peas
1/2 tsp. salt
2 Tbs. butter
2 Tbs. Parmesan cheese

Sauté onion and parsley in melted butter. Add rice and water. Reduce heat and simmer, covered, about 15 minutes or until liquid is gone. Cook peas; drain well. Stir peas, salt and 2 Tbs. butter into rice. Sprinkle with Parmesan cheese.

109. Rice salad. This is a favorite! Can be served hot or cold.

You will need:
1 Tbs. oil
2 cloves garlic, minced
1 medium red or white onion, sliced thin
1-1/2 c. brown rice
2 c. broth of choice

1 tsp. chili powder
1/2 c. halved olives (optional)
1 green pepper, chopped
1 tomato, chopped
Heat oil, add onion and garlic, sauté. Add rice, cook, stirring, about 3 minutes. Add chili powder and broth. Reduce heat and simmer covered till rice is tender, about 45 minutes. Add everything else.

110. *Rice pudding*. Why don't we make this anymore? You can add raisins, nuts, chocolate chips, just about anything to this and make it fun; it is already comforting.

You will need
2 c. cooked rice
1 Tbs. soft butter
1-1/3 c. milk
1 tsp. vanilla
1/2 c. brown sugar
2-4 eggs
dash salt
Combine all ingredients except rice. Add rice. Put in 8" x 8" baking dish, bake for around 50 minutes at 325°F. Serve hot or cold. This is a good crockpot dish.

Beans. Beans take more work, because you have to soak them. Try a practice run right now. Open a cupboard. Take out a container. Pour in some dried beans. Pour water over the beans. See, that wasn't so hard!

Now that the work is taken out of it, let's talk about the beans. They are really, really good for you, they are *filling*, and they are cheap!

111. *Seven-layer bean dip*. This came from our friend Carol. I sometimes have a four-layer bean dip if I don't have all the ingredients! (Recipe is less expensive as I eliminate layers.) I make this

over and over for company. It is a crowd pleaser! Serve with chunks of bread, chips, or vegies.

You will need:

In an 8" x 8" dish, layer in order:

1. refried beans *
2. 1 c. plain yogurt mixed with packet of taco seasoning
3. chopped tomato or salsa
4. chopped black olives
5. cut-up scallions or onions
6. shredded cheddar to barely cover
7. sliced avocado or guacamole**

Refrigerate. Pig out.

* I find good sales on no-fat refried beans in a can. I sometimes make my own, though, which has fat:

Cook 1 c. dried pinto beans in 2-1/2 c. water along with 1 minced garlic clove, 1/3 c. chopped onion, 1 Tbs. shortening, 1 tsp. salt, dash of pepper. Drain when cooked, add to 1/4 c. hot shortening in skillet, mash with potato masher while cooking.

** If using guacamole, make it layer #3. Spreads easier.

112. Classic bean soup.

You will need:

2 c. dried small white beans

1 ham bone

7 c. water

salt to taste

1 Tbs. oil

1/2 c. chopped onion

1 garlic clove, minced

1 bay leaf

Sort and soak beans overnight. Drain beans, add to water and ham bone in big pot. Sauté garlic and onion in oil till tender; add to beans. Add seasoning, bring to boil, reduce heat, simmer covered 2 or more hours. Remove the bone and bay leaf but save any meat for the soup. Remove a cup of the soup and puree in blender to thicken; return to soup, heat 15 minutes more.

113. *Lentil or split pea soup.* So healthy your body will dance a jig!

You will need:

1 medium onion, chopped
2 medium carrots, chopped
1 celery stalk, chopped
oil for sautéing
1 lb. lentils or split peas
1 bay leaf
1 large potato, diced
salt and pepper to taste
8 c. water
1 ham bone

In large pot heat some oil; sauté onion, carrot, and celery. Sort and rinse lentils or peas. Put everything else in pot and bring to boil; cover and simmer till tender, about 1 hour. Remove bone and bay leaf; save any meat for the soup.

114. *Mexican casserole.* This is a good recipe for wild game.

You will need:

1/2 lb. ground meat
1/2 c. minced onion
1 tsp. salt
dash pepper
2 c. cooked pinto beans, drained
1 can tomatoes, undrained
1 garlic clove, minced
1 can diced green chilies (optional)
1/2 tsp. cumin
2 tsp. chili powder
1/2 tsp. oregano
6 corn tortillas
1 8 oz. can tomato sauce
1 c. shredded cheese

Brown meat. Drain all but 1 Tbs. drippings. Sauté onion; add meat, salt, pepper, beans; stir. In saucepan, combine tomatoes, chilies, garlic, cumin, chili powder, oregano, and tomato sauce. Heat to boiling; reduce heat, cover and simmer 10 minutes. Soften tortillas in microwave or by frying briefly. Spread thin layer of sauce on bottom of a two-quart rectangular pan. Top with 3 tortillas, spread with half the bean/meat mixture, pour on more sauce to cover, sprinkle with half the cheese. Repeat, ending with layer of cheese. Bake 30 minutes at 350°F. Give it a few minutes to set when it is done.

115. Hummus. Seasoned correctly, this is a ridiculously inexpensive and delicious dip for breads and vegies. We use hummus and sprouts on sandwiches. Jesus probably dipped bread into a version of hummus, maybe like this one:

You will need:
1 c. drained, cooked chickpeas (garbanzos)
1/4 c. or so reserved cooking water
2 cloves garlic
1/2 tsp. salt
1/2 tsp. cumin
3 Tbs. lemon juice

Puree everything until smooth; then add 1/2 c. loosely packed chopped fresh parsley or 1/4 c. dry parsley flakes. Add water as needed to make dip the right consistency.

116. Ten things to do with a can of pork and beans:

- Eat as is.
- My sister Anne (the "Pork 'n' Bean Queen") mixes a can with leftover rice, wraps the mixture with some shredded cheese in flour tortillas, microwaves for a minute or two, and serves with taco sauce.
- Laura makes chili: 1 can beans, 1 can of stewed tomatoes or tomato sauce, 1/4 lb. browned ground beef, with small chopped onion or dried onion.
- From a magazine recipe card: To 1 can beans add cut-up ham or pieces of lunch meat, crushed pineapple, 1/2 tsp.

dried mustard and 2 Tbs. molasses. Bake at 350°F for 30 minutes.

- Indoor camp food: 1 can of beans, 4 hot dogs, barbecue sauce, refrigerated crescent rolls. Separate rolls into seamless rectangles, mix beans with sauce, spread middle of each rectangle with 1/4 c. beans, put hot dog on each, pinch to close. Bake 20 minutes at 350°F.
- Soup: Add 1 can water to 1 can pork and beans, add small pieces of hot dogs and a little minced onion, 1 Tbs. yellow mustard.
- Baked beans: 1 can of beans, a couple slices of crisp bacon, 1/2 c. chopped onion, 2 Tbs. brown sugar, 2 Tbs. chili sauce, 1 tsp. mustard, salt, some onion. Combine everything. Bake 45 minutes in covered casserole at 350°F.
- Friend Joe adds grated cheddar and heats in a skillet. Best over a campfire, he says.
- Put a toothpick in each one and call it an hors d'oeuvre!
- Donate several cans to your local food bank.

THREE

Clever Gift Giving

Are you happiest when you are *giving*, whether a gift or a hug? Have you prowled around your house looking for something to jazz up a package or add punch to holiday giving? If you are looking for inexpensive gift ideas, make a cup of tea, put up your feet, and read on.

Giftwrap with verve. Who needs the expensive kind? Use a little stored-up creativity:

117. *Keep anything that can be used to wrap a package.* Save paper from gifts received, tissue paper, even protective liners that come on certain products.
118. *Wrap gifts in Sunday funnies or in plain newsprint.* Red ribbon goes particularly well with newspaper. Use hair spray on funnies for gloss.
119. *Wrap small items with attractive magazine pages.*
120. *Use leftover fabric to wrap a gift.* I have odd scraps of calico that I use for everything from basket-liners to tops of canning jars.
121. *Alissa uses wallpaper as gift wrap.* She buys inexpensive odd rolls at the paint store. Yards of nice heavy wrap.
122. *Keep anything that can be used to adorn a package, a basket, or a jar.* Be realistic about this (don't over-accumulate) as well as creative. Use colorful buttons and bells. I keep a decorating stash in one bureau drawer.

123. *Put small presents inside balloons:* coins, small wrapped candies. *Caution:* Balloons, small presents, and small children do not mix!
124. *Always have curly ribbon.* Nothing perks up a present (or a plastic bag) like curly ribbon. Give someone a bag of cookies tied with different colored ribbons with bells on the ends.
125. *When giving food, write the recipe on an index card,* punch a hole in the corner, attach with a ribbon. Presentation!
126. *Attach a small, inexpensive trinket that hints of the gift.* For a baby? Attach a rattle. For a cook, how about a whisk?
127. *Paint a wishbone* with nailpolish and use it to adorn a present.
128. *No ribbon?* Use yarn. *No yarn?* Use string.
129. *Wrap a house gift in a bright, new dishtowel.*
130. *Decorate plain wrapping paper* with stickers and colorful marking pens.
131. *Keep a couple of different-sized baskets on hand* as containers for any kind of gift. Thrift stores sell baskets. Curly ribbon hanging from the basket handle makes a mighty pretty presentation!

Greeting cards. What do you do with the greeting cards you receive? Much too pretty to throw away! Some ideas for recycling:

132. *Homemade postcards!* If a card has no writing on back of the design, cut off the message half of the card and—voila!—instant postcard.
133. *Gift decoration!* At Christmastime I cut the outline of a beautiful nativity scene off a card, wrap a present with plain paper, and glue the picture on top. What a spectacular presentation! (Even if the gift isn't so hot.)
134. *Make name tags for place settings or gifts.*
135. *Make bookmarks, recipe cards, note cards.* Cut in half and use the unwritten side.
136. *Make your own greeting cards.* This is one of our favorite things to do. At our house, this means humor! Magazines, catalogs,

and junk mail end up on the table, along with construction paper. Soon paper is all over the floor and we are giggling.

Fold construction paper in half, booklike. To your "pages" paste pictures and clippings, and compose humorous verse as you go. Bind with string, yarn, or ribbon. You will create many a "masterpiece," and honor the person who gets your work of art.

137. *Don't buy special occasion cards ever again!* Keep a supply of blank cards or pretty note paper for thank you notes, sympathy cards, birthday greetings, or correspondence. Customize the cards with Scripture or favorite prayers.

Take the dread out of birthdays. Here are some ideas to get the creative juices flowing:

138. *Generic birthday gift idea:* Write a special prayer, using the person's name. Send a copy of the prayer on a card (preferably homemade). Announce that you will pray the prayer every day for a specific period, perhaps a month—or even a year! I am fond of a petition in the *Book of Common Prayer:*

> *Watch over thy child,* (child's name), *O Lord, as her days increase; bless and guide her wherever she may be. Strengthen Leslie when she stands; comfort her when discouraged or sorrowful; raise her if she falls; and in her heart may thy peace which passeth understanding abide all the days of her life; through Jesus Christ our Lord. Amen.*

139. *Special birthday idea for a child.* We do this yearly for our two nieces, Olivia and Leah. We call it their "Special Day":

We mail the Birthday Girl a card that offers different choices for her special day, so she can custom-tailor her celebration. This really is her special day and we do everything she wants, within reason.

The day begins with breakfast in a restaurant where we present her with a piggy bank that we have filled with coins during the past year. As she counts her money, we put an envelope on the table and help her separate 10 percent of it as a tithe, to give to God's work. The balance of the money is taken directly to her savings account.

When each girl turned seven we explained the importance of a servant's heart and offered "servant" choices for her next stop. Olivia, who is now ten, chose the Montana Veteran's Home. She and I have gone to visit three times. Once, she quietly held the hand of a man with sunken eyes and a faraway stare. Another time, she squealed on the lap of a veteran while I boogied his wheelchair to the music of Dolly Parton. She was thanked for her small donation by wise staff members who recognized the powerful little heart behind her gift.

This year Leah turned seven. She chose to visit our County Animal Shelter. I raced to the desk ahead of my niece to explain the reason for our visit. "Why, I have just the job for you, Leah," responded a pleasant young man. "How would you like to walk some puppies for us?" It was grand! We had puppy smells on our clothes all day.

We have danced under municipal lawn sprinklers with the girls until we squished when we walked. We have visited radio stations, used book stores, McDonald's for fries, fancy restaurants for breakfast. We have marched through malls and tried to keep up with melting ice cream cones. We've made special memories. Special girls, special days.

140. *Bodacious birthday cakes!* Make small cakes. Buy small plates at thrift stores for a dime. Make a few of these cakes at a time. Extras go in the freezer. Here comes the fun: Custom-decorate these tiny cakes as the birthdays roll round. All frozen frosting comes out, all bureau drawers get flung open, all your creative juices start flowing! DO THIS. Everyone should have a birthday cake:
   - Remember my fisherman friend? I made him a cake with a giant fish hook on top and a "Gone Fishin'" sign made with paper and a toothpick.

- Wrap a ribbon around the cake like a hatband and scatter colored candies and coconut on top.
- Dust confectioners' sugar over doilies for a pretty pattern when you remove the doily (carefully!).
- Drizzle chocolate over the cake until it looks like a work of art.

141. *Give a gift of tradition.* I like making traditions. Sweet rolls for the people at Joe's office on his birthday is a tradition. For MY birthday? The day off. I do not work on my birthday. No one should. If I were president, I'd make it law.

142. *Give savings bonds.* Joshua purchases a birthday savings bond for his godson and namesake. Think about the value of this gift when little Josh is considering college.

143. *Give your time and attention.* One year things were really tough. I cut index cards in half, decorated the edges, used pretty stickers, and wrote a pledge or sentiment on each card. It was my husband's 33rd birthday. I gave him 33 cards. "One backrub, on demand" was his favorite.

Plan ahead. It takes some effort, but it saves some effort later—and money:

144. *Buy gifts on sale throughout the year.* Be alert. Think ahead. One year I began my Christmas shopping in July and felt as if I'd lost weight during the holiday season. The usual heavy burden wasn't there… know what I mean?

145. *Buy inspirational books when waaay reduced in price.* Just a few. They are perfect for last-minute gift-giving to a variety of people.

146. *Keep a "gift box"* into which you put everything from free samples to gift-worthy items, such as coffee mugs. Helps in an emergency!

147. *Give special Christmas ornaments to family or friends.* For half price, you can buy high-quality ornaments the first sale day

after Christmas. Save them until next year or give them as an after-Christmas gift. Tip: If you have small children or are a grandparent I urge you to consider this idea. Josh, now age 24, has a collection beginning with his first Christmas. It is a treasure.

148. *Put away a child's favorite toy when interest wanes. Present it when the child is grown.* It will have sentimental value and perhaps monetary worth.

149. *Buy at season closeout prices for later.* Les buys out-of-season baby clothes at reduced prices to give at baby showers. New moms like to have clothes the baby can grow into. (See "Retail Dateline" in chapter 5.)

Romantic notions. These are gifts that keep on giving:

150. *Plant a tree on your anniversary.* Watch it grow. Sit under its shade when you are old.

151. *Give each other roses for Mother's and Father's Day.* Not the kind that cost as much as your microwave—the kind you plant. Plan your rose garden. Make a rustic arbor out of materials you scrounge up. Plant old roses that climb fences.

152. *Our "gift sack":* Joe and I try to give each other gifts often. We have a white bag, on which is printed "Isle of View" (*"I love you"*). The holder of the sack is responsible to ante up the gift. We give things like favorite candy bars, love notes, even flowers. We try to "sneak" our sack attack so there is mystery and surprise.

153. *Celebrate special days in special ways.* Joe and I eat breakfast for dinner on May 7, the anniversary of our first meeting—which was at breakfast time.

154. *Develop a tradition.* We enjoy a catalog that offers rustic home decor. We make one purchase from this catalog each year, as a mutual anniversary present. One year we could only afford a $7 spatula! Last year we bought a wind chime.

Food gifts. These are limited only by your imagination. You might like to try some of my favorite ideas:

155. *Homemade bread or coffee cake.* Can't be beat.

156. *Brownies Plus!* Here is what I do: I find an 11" x 7" baking pan in a thrift store, bring it home and scour it with steel wool. I make a batch of "Mama's Brownies," wrap them individually in plastic wrap, and fill the shiny pan with brownies, adding a recipe card. (Be sure to tell the recipient that the success of these brownies depends on using this special pan!)

    These are terrific treats! I found the recipe in Mama's collection after she died.

    Mama's Brownies
    2 eggs
    1 c. sugar
    1 tsp. vanilla
    1/2 c. melted butter
    6 Tbs. baking cocoa + 2 Tbs. oil
    1/2 c. flour
    dash salt
    1/2 c. chopped walnuts

    Beat eggs till thick and lemony. Add sugar and beat well. Stir in vanilla, cocoa mixture, melted butter. Mix well. Fold in flour, salt and walnuts. Pour into a greased 11" x 7" pan. Bake 20-25 minutes at 350°F, until you get a little "spring" when you touch it. Important: Let it set for 10 minutes, then cut into squares in pan; let it set for 10 more minutes, then remove to cool on racks.

157. *An apple a day...* Buy a round apple corer/slicer gadget for a couple of dollars. Buy a basket and a cloth napkin at a thrift shop. Line the basket with the napkin (or some old calico or Easter grass). Add nice apples and the slicer. Attach ribbon to the handle. People like gifts of food!

158. *Twelve Months of Christmas.* On the first month of Christmas my dear friend gave to me.... tralalala! Need a *WONderful* pre-

sent for someone special? Do what we did! Make a homemade card that promises food gifts for every month of the year. (Make sure you follow through!) This is what we gave:

January—2 loaves of bread, casserole
February—2 loaves of bread, cookies, and scones
March—stew, brownies, cornbread
April—Italian cookies
May—cheesecake
June—2 coffee cakes, 2 quick breads
July—picnic
August—salad, fruit kuchen, bread
September—canned fruit
October—cake, cookies, soup
November—2 loaves of bread, chili
December—candy, popcorn balls, cheese nip treats

(You might only give one item each month. Ours was for someone very special!)

159. Popcorn balls. Good anytime of year:

You will need:

popcorn to fill a roaster pan about 3/4 full
1 16-oz. package of marshmallows
2 sticks butter

Melt butter and marshmallows together in heavy pan, stirring often. Pour over popcorn; mix well. Let cool slightly. Grease your hands and form into balls.

160. "Popcorn-krispy treats." Ever made those marshmallow-and-rice-cereal treats? Try doing it with popcorn. Cheaper.

161. Cheese treats. This stuff is GOOD!

You will need:

1 box generic cheese crackers
1 box oyster crackers
1/2 c. oil (good use for leftover popcorn oil)
1 package buttermilk dressing mix
dill weed and lemon pepper to taste

Dump everything into a big plastic bag, mix well, and store overnight. (Put it inside a paper grocery bag in case the oil springs a leak.)

Anytime gift ideas. Good ideas for women who like to put that extra love and effort into gifts:

162. *Give the gift of time.* Babysit for a friend, clean someone's house, substitute at work. Relieve someone of a responsibility. What a gift!... Anyone out there want to type for me?

163. *Be generous with your possessions.* We often entertain strangers in our home, some of whom are from other countries. A walk through our house usually turns up a book (maybe about Montana?) or a belonging that is gift-worthy. Look, Jesus said things rust and rot anyway, right?

164. *Give balloons!* People LOVE balloons! Give balloons and cookies as a special cheer-me-up.

165. *Someone just get home from the hospital?* Don't send flowers—send dinner.

166. *Someone IN the hospital?* Don't send flowers—send a note that says you have cleaned her home, watered her plants, walked her dog.

167. *Give a gift certificate to someone's favorite store.* Best bet: Ask a family member to register at a favorite store. Might be a bookstore, a kitchen gadget shop, a clothing store. Then your gifts will be just what they want.

168. *Personalized crafts.* I occasionally cross-stitch. I found a pattern called "Baby" that has a diaper pin built into the design. So for a baby gift, I routinely stitch "Baby" and add the name of the newborn, along with birthdate. I glue felt on the back and frame the whole thing. I bet you could do something similar for a wedding (not with a "Baby" design, however!).

169. *Gift idea for a child:* Find a heavy jar. Fill it with colored rocks. Wrap a ribbon around it. Magic.

170. Decorated T-shirts. For the craft-oriented woman.

You will need:

several dark, good quality T-shirts (thrift store) bleach, water, spray bottle
heavy paper or cereal box cardboard for patterns
scissors
iron
freezer paper (one side shiny)

What you do: Make designs in any size you like (need not be cowboy motif) like cactus, boots, stars, bucking horse. Make patterns with heavy paper or light cardboard. Trace them onto the freezer paper and cut out. Iron shiny side down on your T-shirt, any way you like. You might only want one or two designs in a corner. Put the T-shirt on a protected table and spritz evenly with 1/2 c. bleach mixed with 1/2 c. water. Don't worry if you drip, it adds to the effect. Don't saturate the shirt, just give a nice "dusting." Let sit awhile, then wash in your machine or by hand. Peel the paper off. Say to yourself, "Wow!"

FOUR

Hands-Down Hospitality

I was at a craft show, wandering down aisle after aisle of homemade gadgets and knick-knacks. Weavings, paintings, and photos were stacked and hung everywhere. Then a simple frame and graceful calligraphy drew me toward a gem of ancient wisdom from the Talmud: "Hospitality is an expression of divine worship." Time to dig for the rainy-day money; I had to bring it home! I positioned my find on a wall to be the first thing my guests see.

As Christians, we know that we serve others as a demonstration of our devotion to the Master. Our hospitality toward others can be an aspect of our worship. Jesus will someday say to the people on His right, "For I was hungry and you gave me something to eat, I was thirsty and you gave me something to drink, I was a stranger and you invited me in" (Matthew 25:35).

"SIT LONG, TALK MUCH..."

So says a sign over our table. Do you sit around the table and talk? I wonder if we have drifted too far from this comfortable practice. I bet Jesus had some of his most intimate talks with disciples this way.

I can picture Him, can't you? Oil wicks flickering, Martha running around cleaning everything, Peter wanting to comment about everything, Nathanael sitting there pondering everything, Lazarus laughing. Picture them sitting and laughing, sharing the kind of time friends share when life brings them together for a season, the room peaceful and settled and right. Yes, sit long, talk much. Everything is very right, indeed, when you are with friends.

Entertaining children. Not everyone lives on a lake or has an outdoor area where children can go exploring. But we all have the capacity to entertain children in some way. Our dogs go ballistic when children visit. "Here we are! Here we are!" Their tails wag like propellers. "Come with us! Come with us!" And they are off. The kids, the dogs… sometimes the ***mud***! Here are a few indoor ideas for when kids visit you:

171. *Be equipped for creative endeavors.* Keep coloring books, crayons, paint, and paper on hand for young visitors.
172. *Be a "doll."* Collect an assortment of rag dolls from the thrift store and give children their pick when they visit.
173. *Always include children if you're cooking.* I have a sturdy stool for their kitchen use. Children are conscripted to serve appetizers, set the table, help cook. They love it and so do I.
174. *Keep an assortment of videos for children of all ages.* Purchase videos inexpensively when rental stores retire them.
175. *Make a visit into a party!* Save toilet paper rolls, fill with candy, wrap with Sunday funnies, tie ends with string: party favors! Also nice to put on a visiting child's plate at dinner.
176. *Keep a candy basket just for the kids.* I found a homemade, long-necked "Mother Goose" basket-cover. Small hands eagerly reach under one of her wings to grab a treat.
177. *Throw a do-it-themselves party for kids!* Divide kids into three groups. Group 1 = the cooks. Supervise a "spaghetti brigade": pasta, canned sauce, garlic bread, salad, and juice from concentrate make an easy meal. Group 2 = decorators. Encourage the children to be creative and don't panic as they rummage through your drawers. Ask them to set a pretty table and then turn them loose, inside and out. Try to have a good supply of

balloons in an obvious spot. Group 3 = entertainers. Help them by offering paper and pencil for planning, the use of musical instruments, the liberty of ransacking closets for costumes and other supplies as they need them. This group also writes a grace with emphasis on the birthday child or other guest of honor.

You supervise. You will never be disappointed with the results! Neither will the children.

Dining. How many times have you said, "Oh no, thank you, I wouldn't think of letting you help; after all, you are my guest, blahblahblah." I like to pitch in and DO something when I'm the guest! Yet I am stuck in the living room with the husbands. Phooey.

178. *Next time people ask if they can help, find something they can do!* I've even pulled men into the kitchen. It's fun; makes people feel at home.

179. *Sponsor a potluck picnic.* Tell everyone to bring whatever they want. You'll have an interesting meal. You supply the beverage, and utensils.

180. *Do a special dinner for someone.* Long ago I purchased a toaster-sized box full of recipe cards. Hundreds of cards. I made it my goal to prepare every one of those recipes (except calves' brains). It's my hobby. I am 75 percent through. We put stickers on the cards and evaluate results. Some have been rip-roaring disasters. Grim remembers two: Boston Cream Rock and Black Bottom Soup.

Sometimes we put a red ribbon on the box and deliver it to a special friend. That person picks a meal in honor of a birthday or anniversary. The only catch: Pick recipes never cooked before. And no brains. We often go to our friend's house to prepare the meal, and sometimes we do this for others at our home.

"What do you do if it's a flop?" asked our friend Jackie. We laugh and defrost a pizza. Remember the commandment on attitude.

181. *Make special desserts for special people.* I bought a 225-page dessert cookbook. It just sat with all my other cookbooks that just sit. One day we took it off the shelf and wrote this inside the front cover:

Dear Friend,
Cookbooks, like friendships, sometimes sit on shelves and don't get used. Let's do something about that! Would you kindly look through this book and choose a recipe that appeals to you? Return the book, make note of the recipe, and we will prepare it for you. Joe & Cynthia

182. *Host a theme dinner.* We don't get bogged down with routine around here! We eat Sri Lankan-style without utensils; we have open-house Italian Sundays. We have Super Bowl parties, Polish dinners, and sushi smorgasbords!

183. *One of our favorites was a theme dinner built around a movie.* A popular children's movie, *The Black Stallion*, portrays life in the 1930s. We researched clothing styles and recipes popular in that era and sent invitations to friends asking them to bring a dish (recipe included) and wear clothes that fit the time. We all watched the movie and ate a comforting meal, dressed in charming clothes. We are planning the sequel, which is set in the Middle East. I have already picked my costume. Maybe we'll eat without utensils.

Other parties and games. Here are a few more ideas:

184. *Plan an adult treasure hunt.* Treasure hunts can become competitive! Our pastor and my mother nearly landed in jail a few years ago because of a treasure hunt! I list simple things—like Polish catechisms, tutus, water from Niagara Falls.... Make lists, send people off in cars or on foot, gather everyone for judging at a specified time, present awards. We give terrific awards, like quart jars of prune juice.

185. *Do you play board games around your table?* Good!

186. *Try a Murder Mystery party.* We host them for teens and adults. Great fun. (Buy used games at a thrift store.)

Take-out hospitality. The focus is on others:

187. *Preschool mamas.* Organize a play group with other mothers home with children. Invite them and their brood to your home one morning a week, perhaps from ten o'clock to noon. Mothers have the choice of staying and visiting or using the time for errands. Next week, a different mom hosts the group. This is cheap babysitting and an opportunity to exchange ideas with other mothers.

188. *Invite a missionary or foreign exchange student to your home.* Prepare a "comfort food" for your guest. Have your children draw and color the flag representing your guest's country.

189. *Do something for your pastor.* Just out of seminary, Thad and his wife Lori came to our church. They had begun a family. They were up to their ears in responsibility: church issues, church concerns, church problems. Pastors do not have cushy lives.

    We decided to swap houses for an evening. Joe and I went to their home, fed their two little ones, and spent the night. They came to our house. To solitude. We had a meal ready and the table set, with strict instructions to leave the dirty dishes. This was a time of peace for them, a time to catch their breath, a time of utmost privacy.

190. *Visit a nursing home.* Don't forget about the elderly.

    Once I took several small children to visit a local nursing home. We brought our pet cat, a little dog, and a new lamb. There was a certain man at the nursing home. He didn't move. He didn't talk. He had no expression. He just sat in his chair. With innocence I covet, a young girl marched up to his chair with the lamb. The animal was wild-eyed and nervous, but quieted as if hearing a command from an unseen source.

    The old man placed his enormous hand on the head of the

lamb. Tears welled in his eyes. He never spoke a word. He didn't have to.

When Josh was a baby I took him to the county old folks home. I put him on the floor and he crawled from bed to bed. "Get that child off the floor! Where's his mother? Come here, little boy!" Joshua wasn't a year old, yet he brought joy to bedridden women, just by crawling on the floor.

191. Remember others in little ways. My mother taught me to bring a cool drink to anyone working near our home. Utility men and road crews still benefit from the lesson I learned as a child.

FIVE

Skirting the Cost: Fashion on a Shoestring

Linen or polyester, plain or polka-dot, clothes are things that few women have the time, talent, or ambition to make. I admire women who do. If it was up to me to sew their clothing, my family would be covered in trash bags. A couple of slits here and there, durable, waterproof, and the latest in decorator green!

For those of us without time, talent or ambition to sew, this chapter talks about clothing purchase and maintenance, and presumes that you want to save money in the process.

The commandment on attitude kicks in here. If you are embarrassed to go to a thrift shop, or timid to ask questions in a department store, you might be stuck buying clothes at "Manufacturer's Suggested Retail Price!" You don't want to do that, do you? I sure don't! I can offer a few pointers to help you overcome embarrassment and redirect your clothing budget to something else... maybe that overdue vacation!

RETAIL STORES

Two factors mark success for any retail store: good markup and high turnover of merchandise. There is, however, one significant difference between discount and department stores, and that is in purchasing methods.

Discount stores. Mike once worked for a large retail chain and this is what he told me: Discount stores have buyers who purchase merchandise for large blocks of stores at once. Since the merchandise is centrally bought and warehoused, it is automatically shipped to each store along with a marketing strategy.

Merchandise decisions are based on factors such as economy, previous sales, and marketing thrust. A team of buyers meets to assess last year's sales. Ads and promotionals are geared toward items that are historically successful or are new and show promise.

Discounters rely on a good "marriage" between their marketing and buying departments. Discount stores operate on a smaller margin than department stores. This is due to several factors: large volume, reduced salary cost, lower markup than department stores, and national advertising.

Department stores. Corporate retailers, or department stores, depend on department managers to order merchandise, based primarily on past sales and trends in the fashion industry. Each department manager is responsible for all ordering and must make an "assortment plan" of merchandise in preparation for seasons and holidays.

Most department store retailers plan for 60 percent or higher markup. This leaves plenty of room for sales offers. For the most part, inventory must be liquidated at each store. Excess inventory is not stored for next year! This translates to a department manager needing savvy and wisdom (and maybe a bit of luck) in devising the assortment plan.

Sales. What is a sale? To some people it is the equivalent of the cavalry's "Charge!" (Regrettably, for many that is *exactly* what it means!) Mike explained the term "sale" is not the same as "clearance." When something is on sale, it is reduced in price and often goes back up again. Nearly everything in most stores is marked 25 percent off at one time or another.

Is there really such a thing as "Manufacturer's Suggested Retail

Price?" To call it a gimmick would not be fair, but neither is the notion that manufacturers can legally tell retailers what to charge. Retailers determine price based on cost to them, marketing, freight, and overhead.

Retail dateline. Are you amused when you see bathing suits on sale before the snow melts, school clothes on display while you are basking by the pool, and ski boots advertised when you are raking leaves? Welcome to the retail dateline! Retailers celebrate July 4 at Easter, winter in summer, and Halloween on Labor Day. If a store has to be 100 percent "back-to-school" by July, the racks of bathing suits, beach towels, and shorts have got to go. But they have ***no place to send them!*** Aha! Chances are, you will end up with "summer clothes drastically reduced" starting around the beginning of July! Get it?

192. ***Want a general guideline to the dateline?*** Start watching for spring clothing closeouts around the last week in April. Watch for any holdover spring, as well as all summer clothing, to close out around the last week in July. Most fall and all back-to-school clothes should close out around the end of October, while winter clothes and the holiday season get slashed around the end of January.

"Clean Up in Season" is a sacred phrase in retail. It means items with a seasonal application must be sold during that season or holiday time. Take Valentine's Day, the most costly day for retail stores. It is hard to buy inventory for this holiday. Why? What's a merchant to do with two dozen heart-shaped boxes of candy—on the 15th of February?

A good department store will be out of seasonal merchandise at the peak of the season. If you wait until "out-of-stock" price slashing, the nice selection will be long gone. However, retailers reduce prices dramatically on goods that have lingered beyond the peak selling period.

If you are patient, trips with your list to the mall (several department stores) during any of the projected out-of-stock sales will probably net you a terrific buy. What a great opportunity to buy

Christmas or birthday gifts at significant savings! Why not buy a snowsuit two sizes too large for baby so it fits perfectly next year? My friend Sharon was able to buy an expensive pair of athletic shoes for under $10. That is smart shopping!

What are your designs on? Is it frugal to wear designer clothes? Good question. The answer depends on whether you are interested in quality or fashion. Can you have both? Yes. And because of that there is validity in paying a bit more for something. But some design labels merely present a "specific look," which, of course, is discarded like yesterday's trash as soon as a new look comes along.

193. *Think "timeless," not "dated."* No matter where you buy clothes, opt for timeless, classic styles that will survive each new season's fashion industry assault. (For example, one necessary outfit: excellent-fitting slacks or skirt, crisp white blouse, and blazer.) Learn to accessorize and use color to your advantage. Add good posture, a confident gait, a look-someone-in-the-eye smile, and you will dazzle us all!

Most of my clothes sport a "quality" label. My clothes wear well, look good, and hold up to washing. Nearly all of my clothes come from thrift stores.

THRIFT STORES

"O vanity! Thy name is woman!" **Hamlet**

Yes, at times I am sheepish about parking outside the thrift store. The sheepishness wears off fast, though, when I tote home my loot. I wish I could take you on a tour of my closet. Designer labels and quality clothes. Clothes I could never buy at full retail: shoes, coats, skirts, sweaters, blouses, dresses, and pants. Joe's side mirrors mine: sportcoats, boots, sweaters. Josh, too! If there is a thrift store nearby, give it a try.

But keep your sense of humor. Once, feeling particularly romantic, I decided to shop at "my" store for a negligee to dazzle my husband. Sure enough, I found a stunning teal nightgown with matching robe for only $2.29. I raced home, quickly laundered my find, bathed from head to foot, coiffed my hair, spritzed on perfume, put on the outfit, and swept into the bedroom. Joe gasped in dismay.

I caught a glimpse in the mirror. We burst out laughing. I looked like the Queen of the Dorks! I took the outfit back. I bought two baskets for one dollar and had $1.29 to spare. A peach cardigan caught my eye. The tag said $1.29. Perfect! I snapped it up. At home I looked at the label. My eyes widened when I read the designer name! The tag read: "100 percent silk." I put it on. It was beautiful. When I put my hand in the pocket I found the original price tag. This gorgeous brand-new designer sweater had cost someone $150!

WHERE DO YOU START?

Open your closet door. (Have hubby and kids do the same.) Stand there awhile and look. What don't you wear? Kick it out! Now take a look at the clothes you wear most. Does the style and color really suit you? If not, kick it out! (This is a book about thrifty living? Stick with me!)

Look at what is left. Simple black dress? Red dress? Can you wear a scarf, jewelry, a wide belt, a narrow belt, a vest, a sweater, a tunic with the dress? Do you see a pair of pants? How many different blouses or sweaters can you wear with them? Can you sew a cluster of buttons on a collar? Can you tie a scarf around your waist? Use what you have! Be creative! Adjust your attitude! Roll up your sleeves... literally!

Figure out what you need to make your basic wardrobe complete. Determine how much you will spend for an item. (Know your prices!) Make a list. Make as many items interchangeable as possible. And ask yourself some questions: "Do I really need five coats? Do I really need fourteen pairs of summer shorts? Do I really need nine blazers?"

Keep your list in mind as you haunt garage sales or thrift stores. Church rummage sales are terrific! Take your list to the mall to shop close-out sales. Be patient. Watch. Keep an eye on quality clothing that lingers past peak selling periods. Over time you will find everything. Guaranteed.

Caution! Do not make your list and fly to the mall with a mission! You bought this book because you want to be frugal, right? Demand shopping, impulse shopping, and recreational shopping should be a thing of the past for you. If you want recreation, take a walk. Note from Grim: Don't take this as an invitation to walk to the mall!

$uper $avers

194. Wait and watch. Merchandise is normally displayed thirty days before it is put on sale.

195. Watch and wait. When you find something you want, watch it for a few weeks. If selling fast you must decide if you will pay full retail. Otherwise, wait for the sale. Once it is discounted, check to see if it is moving; watch how many are on the rack. If still in good quantity, it will probably be lowered again—the store is watching, too! If it has not sold and has not been reduced, go to the manager and ask if you can purchase it for a lesser price. In fact, go to the manager whenever you have a problem or question. A good manager is concerned about customer satisfaction. Bottom line: no customer, no store!

196. "Specials" are usually sales for items seldom or never carried before. Often a "this ad only" kind of offer, and usually "loss leaders," they represent a special deal the retailer got from a manufacturer. Traditionally, the quality is poorer than normal merchandise. Want an example? Ever seen men's flannel shirts that sold two for $10? Ever bought them? Ever washed them? Shrunk and lost shape in no time, didn't they?

197. *"Clearance" or "Red Tag Sales" means the goods are being reduced permanently.* The first clearance markdown is usually 30 percent.

198. *One half or more off is usually a good buy.*

199. *Wait for year-end sales.* Stores of all kinds attempt to liquidate inventory before the close of the year—taxes!

200. *Avoid high traffic areas: Impulse items!* This merchandise has the highest markup and is usually the "in" fashion. Best sales are found in the back of the department. Surprise.

201. *"O/S" is good news for you.* "Out of stock" is retail lingo for "It's outta here!"… often at any price.

202. *Risk waiting to do your Christmas shopping.* Unless you've shopped little by little since last January, don't go Christmas shopping until one or two days before Christmas. You are chancing a poorer selection, but during the last few days many quick decisions are made to get rid of inventory.

203. *Give gift certificates for Christmas.* A dollar will purchase as much as twice more the week after Christmas.

204. *Have patience when shopping—both retail and thrift stores.* Thrifty shopping requires repeat visits, strategy, objectivity. Our little thrift store is handy, and I swing through routinely. Many times I leave empty-handed. Sometimes I net spectacular savings on spectacular merchandise.

205. *Develop a routine.* Follow a "route." Over time I have learned where to find best buys, where not to waste time.

206. *Control yourself!* Yes, I come home with unneccessary "bargains." A little like eating past my fill. Not wise, not frugal.

207. *Enough is enough!* When you have all you need, stop shopping! It may be a thrift store, but if you are spending lots of money there regularly you are not being thrifty.

208. *Learn thrift store savvy.* Learn quality. Read labels. Think twice. Look twice. Why is this garment in a thrift store? Is it stained?

Ripped? Buttons missing? Does it require expensive or time-consuming care?

209. *Learn "your" colors.* Color me anything, but I am sure getting sick of red! I am one of those who wear red well. Open my closet and what do you see? Yep. From "see to shining see." Red. And white. White looks good on me, too.

Certain colors and styles look good on you. If you never thought about this, hold different colors up to your face and look in the mirror. You will know in a flash what colors suit you. I cannot go near light brown or beige. Not many people can wear black. Clothing store employees can usually help you determine your personal color scheme.

Stick with colors you know will enhance your overall look, and build a basic wardrobe using those colors. Once you do, you will be able to have a few basic items to mix and match to your heart's content, slashing lots from your clothing allowance.

210. *Go to rummage sales or garage sales.* Especially in upper-crust neighborhoods.

211. *Avoid unnecessary catalog buying.* Catalog buying is usually more expensive, and you can't try anything on. I once bought a long black corduroy shirtdress from a catalog. When I put it on I looked like a Greek olive with feet.

212. *A $50 dress worn often is much more sensible than a $30 dress worn twice.*

213. *Do not buy a new wardrobe!* Accessorize what you have.

214. *Change the buttons on something to give it a new look.* I sometimes sew a cluster of buttons on a cotton blazer or shirt to jazz it up.

215. *Swap clothes with friends or relatives,* especially if you have children. Get together each season and clean out drawers and closets. Use what you have, remember?

216. *Assemble a dynamite outfit for a child or woman in need,* package it nicely, include homemade treats, and send a delegation to deliver this thoughtful gift!

217. *Do your kids need expensive sports equipment?* Do you need a bank loan just to keep the kids in sport shoes? Start a co-op! Use your garage as a sport-shoe consignment shop. Give donated shoes to less fortunate children.

CARE AND MAINTENANCE OF CLOTHING

Just as storage has everything to do with saving money on food, care and repair have everything to do with clothing.

We live in such a disposable society we think nothing of replacing everything we own over and over. Are we not satisfied? Or has Madison Avenue convinced us we aren't normal unless we dress the same as everyone else? Well, phooey! If you know your colors and which styles look good, you will find quality clothes with a classic look that will, indeed, last a lifetime. That sounds pretty frugal to me.

$uper $avers

218. *Take permanent press items out of the dryer at once.* Hang or fold immediately.

219. *Don't use wire hangers for heavy clothing.* If you must, double hangers with masking tape.

220. *Cotton pants too short?* Don't get rid of them yet! Alissa steps on hems while wet and P-U-L-L-S, then line dries. Lots of extra mileage from kids' sweats this way.

221. *Line dry often.* Clothes last longer if kept out of the dryer! Saves on electricity or gas, too.

222. *Cut fabric softener sheets in half.* They'll still be adequate, and they'll go twice as far. (Caution: Some fabric softener sheets leave greasy spots on silk and polyester, which will only come out with dry cleaning.)

223. *Read care labels.* Saves a lot of grief.

224. *Dark colors usually stay newer-looking longer.*

225. *Extend clothing life.* Iron knee patches inside children's pants for longer wear. Stitch around the patch to keep it in place.

226. *Ring around the collar?* Shampoo dissolves body oils.

227. *Clothes fade less if washed inside-out.* Nap stays fresher, too.

228. *Avoid 100 percent cotton shirts.* They are a headache, says Donna, a professional dry cleaner for thirty years. Crisp-looking when starched and ironed, they do not hold their press. She pulled a man's shirt from her rack. It was a splendid-looking blue pinstripe. "Two hours under a sport jacket and this will be wrinkled again." Josh recently bought his first suit at a close-out sale. He was proud to report he also bought a $40 cotton shirt for just $10. What he didn't report was that it was the kind of fabric that wrinkles no matter what you do. He will probably be like the rest of us and put it in a laundry basket for the rest of his natural life. (Sort of like putting a $10 bill on the floor and just... leaving it there.)

229. *Save time <u>and</u> money.* Purchase a good cotton/polyester blend that does not require ironing.

230. *Keep stains off your clothes.* Wear an apron. Get dressed after spraying your hair or applying perfume.

231. *Get a good book on stain removal.* You will soon get your money's worth out of it!

232. *A good antiperspirant will stretch the life of good clothes* if someone in your family has a perspiration problem. Wear dress shields, and tell hubby to wear a T-shirt under his dress shirts.

233. *Air out clothes before putting them away.*

234. *Hang knits, like pants, over a hanger.* They will keep better.
235. *Don't throw wet clothes in a heap*—you will never get the wrinkles out!
236. *Do you have a cat or a dog?* Purchase a good lint roller or carding brush to keep your clothes neat.
237. *Always wash reds alone.* Especially new garments. Is there a man alive who doesn't have at least one set of pink underwear? Joe's are nice. Did I tell you I wear red well?
238. *Avoid mildew!* No one can get rid of mildew.
239. *Try bulk-rate dry cleaning.* Some dry cleaners offer a bulk rate. For example, ten pounds for $12. They pre-treat and dry clean, but you do the ironing. I like that kind of deal.
240. *Avoid "dry clean only" clothing.* To save money, buy what can be washed at home.
241. *Wash woolens carefully if you don't dry clean them.* Once wool shrinks it gets "felted" and cannot be stretched back.
242. *Rayon does not hold up well to home washing.* As a rule, it must be dry cleaned.
243. *Not all silks are alike.* If you buy anything silk, check first to see if it can be washed.
244. *Take advantage of dry cleaning seasonal specials:*
    Spring: drapes, pillows, blankets, spreads
    Fall: hunting clothes, sleeping bags
    Prom time: formals
245. *Shoe repair is worth it.* Always check with your repairman to see if shoes can be repaired.
246. *Replace heels, not shoes.* I have a pair of "fashion" cowboy boots. They are fifteen years old. I wear them often with long skirts. I have replaced the rubber end of the heels several times, at a cost of only $2 each time. The rubber end of the heel is much less expensive to replace than the entire heel. Don't wait too long!

247. *Save shoes by using nylon "taps."* After you wear shoes awhile, bring them to a shoe repair shop. Ask them to figure out where to put nylon taps to save on wear.
248. *Know what's not repairable.* Most children's shoes, says my shoe repairman, are not repairable, nor are cheaper shoes or shoes that are plastic.
249. *Keep leather work boots greased.* Discount stores sell boot grease in the sporting section.
250. *Scuff marks are tough to remove.* Use cream polish on shoes before they get scuffed.
251. *Save old shoes for doing yard work.* Ever cut your grass wearing new sneakers? Oops.
252. *Two ideas for shoe liners/insulators:* Trace the outline of your foot on a styrofoam meat tray and cut to fit your shoe, or use thin carpet scraps to line winter boots.
253. *Buy quality shoes and take care of them,* says Bill the shoe guy. There is a message here, isn't there?

SEWING

Just to prove I'm a good sport, I am going to say a few things about sewing:

- I wish I did. You can save a ton of money if you do.
- You can find better quality zippers or buttons in thrift stores—on clothes!
- Ditto your old clothes: Save buttons and zippers.
- Learn to darn if your family wears wool socks. Or send them to my mother, who's incredible!

SIX

You Are Beautiful

In *The Fragrance of Beauty*, Joyce Landorf inspires women to reflect an inner beauty that comes from the right relationship with God. "The woman, the teen-ager, or the child that can slip easily into prayer has a beauty formula going for her that no cosmetic on the market can beat."

It is a joy to meet women adorned with the fruit of the Spirit: love, joy, peace, patience, kindness, goodness, faithfulness, gentleness, and self-control. This is Christian character produced by the Holy Spirit—and it is beautiful. No cosmetic, diet plan, or health regimen can compete with the holistic power of the indwelling Spirit of God in a virtuous woman! The glow is unmistakable, the smile beatific.

But what if she wants to line that smile with pink, red, or coral? What if she wants to frame that glow with a pretty haircut? How can she be beautiful on the outside, without paying exorbitant prices?

YOU GET WHAT YOU PAY FOR!

We do, indeed, get what we pay for when it comes to beauty and health aids: fancy packaging and heavy advertising. I don't like to pay for those things, so I look for generic or less-expensive products. Some expensive products may be superior, but I am skeptical.

We tend to impulse-buy in the beauty department. We listen to claims, read ads... and seem to be on a never-ending self-improvement cycle. Anything promising results gets our attention!

I urge you to look for less-expensive substitutes for cosmetics and beauty aids. When considering expense, however, compare carefully and consider a few things. Remember the fact that glowing health and beauty are synonymous; we need to take care of ourselves in the first place, not just compensate for all our flaws!

$uper $avers

254. *Take inventory of your bathroom shelves before you make purchases.* Are you going to use that "Wondercream" you are tempted to buy?

255. *Does the more expensive skin-care product come in concentrated form?* Will it last longer than its less costly alternative?

256. *Do you really need that expensive hypo-allergenic make-up?* Will a less expensive product cause skin reaction?

257. *To whiten fingernails:* Soak them in lemon juice, then brush them with an equal amount of white vinegar and warm water; rinse.

258. *Remove make-up easily with baby oil.* Petroleum jelly is another great make-up remover.

259. *Add a little baby oil to your bath water.* Careful, though—tub may become slippery!

260. *Home blemish cream:* Dab a pimple with lemon juice several times a day to dry it out.

261. *Substitute hair conditioner for shaving cream.*

262. *Facials*—an assortment to try:

- Make a strong brew of chamomile tea. Mix 1/2 c. tea with 1 Tbs. olive oil. Apply to face after washing it at night.
- Mash 1/2 avocado (when on sale, of course!). Apply and leave on for 20 minutes; rinse.

- Mix an egg white with some water. Apply to your face and allow to dry until nice and tight; rinse.
- Oily skin: Make a paste of oatmeal and water. Apply and let dry on face; rinse with cool water.
- Blemishes: Smooth honey on face. Leave on 20 minutes; rinse with warm water.

263. *Avoid metal barrettes and rubber bands.* They break hair after repeated use; use cloth bands.

264. *Brushing is good—up to a point.* Brushing helps distribute natural oils in hair, but can be damaging if overdone (roughs up the cuticle).

265. *Wax in your hair?* Many hair conditioners, particularly cream rinses, cause wax buildup. Read labels! Stay clear of waxy-sounding ingredients, such as lanolin.

266. *Too much conditioner buildup?* Wash with a mixture of vinegar or lemon juice and water.

267. *Is it a bargain?* Big bottles of shampoo may look like a bargain, but water is often the main ingredient.

268. *Salon shampoos are concentrated.* Use less! Much less!

269. *Find a beauty salon that will trim neck and bangs between cuts for free.* My hairdresser Beth does this for me, stretching my haircut dollar several extra weeks.

270. *At-home hair coloring can be an inexpensive alternative IF you:* (a) do it right, (b) pick the right color, (c) pick a coloring agent that is compatible with your perm, if you have one. Beth routinely sees women who have blundered at (d) all of the above.

271. *Color—or highlighting?* Beth recommends highlighting instead of color because it lasts longer, camouflages grey, and makes you feel good. She and I debate this regularly because highlighting is costly.

272. *Just don't do it.* Grey is beautiful, too.

273. *Adopt an all-one-length hairstyle to avoid haircuts.*

274. *Do not cut your own bangs,* unless you are practiced. Pay to have this done or turn to a trusted friend.

275. *Johanna makes beautiful hair "scrunchies" for her ponytail with old silk ties.* Thrift shop special!

276. *Highlight blond hair with 1/4 c. lemon juice in 3/4 c. water.* A dose of sunshine makes this process more effective.

277. *Use olive oil to condition dry, brittle hair.*

278. *Clean brushes and combs in a mixture of vinegar or ammonia and water.*

279. *Replace your toothbrush every few months,* getting replacements free from your dentist when you go for your check-up.

280. *"A little dab will do ya."* Teach your children this when they are learning to brush their teeth.

281. *Cut open a tube of toothpaste to get the last smidgen.* Ditto hand-cream. That's after you've already flattened the tube with the side of a pencil or the back of a comb!

282. *Don't buy any kind of diet!* Why pay someone to tell you what you already know? You want to lose weight and you have to discipline yourself to do so. You already know this: Eat as many fruits and vegetables as you can stand, get a good dose of dairy every morning, eat lots of hearty grain products, and drink lots of water. Read Galatians 5:22-23; stand tall, meet everyone with a smile. Don't you feel better already?!

283. *Check to see if the community health department sponsors free medical tests.* Examples: well-baby exams; mammograms; prostate, diabetes, and blood pressure tests.

284. *Ask if generic drugs can be substituted on a prescription.*

285. *Save every medical expense for possible tax deduction,* including mileage to and from the doctor!

286. *Getting new glasses?* Have the old pair tinted for next-to-nothing. Instant prescription sunglasses! Or donate the old pair to the Lions Club.

287. *Sunburn soothers:* Apply cider vinegar. Or try milk of magnesia. I hear the mint-flavored works wonders!

288. *Try baking soda as a deodorant.* Apply with a powder puff.

289. *Use baking soda as a facial scrub.* Rinse with cool water.

290. *When is the last time you soaked your feet?* Talk about a simple pleasure! Very warm water and some baking soda.

A good way to end a day—and a chapter.

SEVEN

Do Buffalo Roam in Your Home?

The Proverbs 31 woman "looks well to the ways of her household" (Prv 31:27). Are there times when you look *away* from your harried household? Regardless of your resolve, does your house get away from you? When you do clean your castle, are money-saving and time-cutting methods critically important? Is there a way around costly convenience? Can you cut your cleaning dollar without having to tackle each task with a chisel and homemade soap? I can offer some friendly experience in this department.

I was active in the business world until I slipped in a tub and hit my head. Temporarily disabled with stuttering, the inability to concentrate, and "spells," the strain of my previous work was too much. What could I do? I could clean people's houses! Before long I built a small business, and I still clean houses, offices, and stores. I learned there is more skill to this craft than I thought, and have blundered my way through many cleaning situations.

HOUSEKEEPING

When most women were at home all day, they could routinely clean, shake, and bake; each day had a special chore. Fast-forward to today's single-parent or nuclear family. Add a full-time job with commute, ferrying the kids to an endless assortment of activities, trying to maintain sound nutrition, recharging your batteries somehow so you can stay awake past 8:00 P.M.—all while the dust accumulates on the VCR, layers of exploded food build up in the microwave, and thick soap scum coats the shower. Whether you are at home during the day or chasing off to work, housekeeping is a big job! And organization is key.

Do a wall a day. Know what I do? I do a wall a day! I begin at a specific spot in my home and clean my way around, following the wall. I clean only a small area each day. When I get to something like a dresser, I clean a drawer a day. If only to pick dead leaves from a floor plant, I always have a section of "wall" on my daily list. And if I don't get to it today, there is always tomorrow.

Get rid of your clutter. Turn to the commandment on using things up. Slash through your trash. If you are not using something, send it packing! There are people in your town who are in need of your excess. I would wager, though, that much of your clutter collection has little value: piles of junk mail, catalogs and magazines, old clothes, new clothes that require more care than you care to give. Roll up your sleeves! Clutter makes work that takes time that we don't have!

One of the first places to eliminate clutter is under the kitchen sink or wherever it is that you keep cleaning supplies. Let's walk over there together, now, you and I.... Okay. We are looking at a couple of nearly empty pump bottles of the blue "window stuff," several dozen rusted scouring pads, a rust-stained cottage cheese container that was supposed to hold the scouring pads, ant and roach spray, assorted spray bottles of "Superpowerclean," the latest miracle toilet bowl cleaner, two or three cans of furniture polish, floor-cleaning gunk, light bulbs, a box of soggy dishwasher detergent, a few partial rolls of paper towels, and 17 empty jars, with or without lids.

Want a project that will lift your spirits? Clean under your sink. Take it all out. Find someplace to store duplicate products. Here is what you should have:

- Dishwashing detergent
- Dishwasher detergent
- Plastic container with copper or stainless steel scouring pads, not those messy things with soap
- One bottle of non-sudsy ammonia
- One bottle of white vinegar
- One small bottle of citrus-based cleaner for grease, scuff marks, etc.
- One spray bottle of homemade window washing liquid (see tip #330).
- One bottle of bleach or soft-bleach cleaner
- Old toothbrushes: one for toilet-cleaning, one for general cleaning
- Commercial-grade floor cleaner
- Baking soda
- Furniture polish
- Assortment of clean rags
- Optional: Commercial-grade soap scum remover (I refuse to live without mine!)

This list is more than you will need to keep your castle sparkling; let it be a goal. First, use everything you have on hand. Don't succumb to advertisers' claims again!

Down on your knees! Invest in rubber gloves. Put them on. Invest in a sponge. Grab it. Grab a toothbrush and your bottle of soft white bleach cleanser. Go kneel down next to your toilet. Flush. Put the bleach on the sponge, get under the rim, wipe down the seats, the entire bowl, the handle. Use the toothbrush on the hinges. This entire process will take less than five minutes. I promise. Note: If you have hard water, it leaves deposits that need an acid cleaner. A commercial phosphoric-acid-based bowl cleaner is safest for you and your toilet.

$uper $avers

291. *Consolidate duplicate cleaning products.*

292. *Buy refills.*

293. *Use rags instead of paper towels.*

294. *Don't buy fancy cleaners,* especially for the toilet bowl. (I am routinely disappointed by highly advertised products. Products with less advertising money are often better—people wouldn't buy them unless they perform.)

295. *Visit a janitor supply shop.* My work takes me to a janitor supply store, and my visits always teach me something new about cleaning. I strongly recommend you visit such a store because it will help you to be frugal! Many commercial products come in concentrated form, are much less expensive overall, and are significantly better in performance than most grocery store supplies. I often learn new cleaning uses for ordinary household supplies.

296. *Use bleach diluted in water to disinfect* if you are not worried about color loss or fading. Be careful! Grim squirted some of this stuff on his pants by accident. I think that's how he got his name.

297. *Price per pound is not a good measure in cleaning products;* it depends on how well they clean.

298. *Cheap detergents have an abundance of filler* (such as salt, the cheapest part of laundry detergent, which softens water). This gives you less cleaning power.

299. *I do not like bar soap.* This is my opinion, an opinion based on cleaning hundreds of bathrooms. It is messy, wasteful, and unsanitary. I like pump soap. I keep dispensers at our kitchen and bathroom sinks, and at the tub. I buy a gallon of refill soap from a warehouse store, at very near the price I paid for the original dispenser. Use up bar soap for decoration or for a sachet in your dresser.

300. *Dust on your coffee table?* Dust on your end table? Dust on your sofa and chairs, too! (Same dust!) Vacuum or wipe clean.

301. *Vacuum your mattress every couple of months.* Invisible mites thrive on flakes of dead skin. Discard your filter bag immediately.

302. *Air out your bedding as often as you can.* This is not only a cheap way to maintain cleanliness in your boudoir, it is better for you!

303. *Run pillows and blankets through "air fluff" in your dryer.* Cuts down cleaning costs.

304. *Best bet for hard floors of any kind:* a commercial quality dust-mop and water-based dust spray. Much easier than sweeping and it gets up more grit.

305. *Use a pH neutral product when damp-mopping; the shine will last longer.* Dirt is acidic, and if you use an alkaline cleaner it will loosen the wax finish.

306. *To strip wax off your floor use ammonia and water,* half and half. Rinse well, then neutralize with vinegar, 1/2 c. to one quart of water. OR use a commercial "rinse free" wax remover—and rinse well.

307. *Never use an acrylic-based product on a no-wax floor!*

308. *Discount stores generally do not carry good grade waxes.*

309. *Wash and wax simultaneously?* You know—those products you squirt on your floor that do it all? Let's think about this for a minute, okay? Where do you think the dirt goes? Do you think that maybe, just maybe, it is picked up, distributed evenly, and firmly locked in place when the wax dries?

310. *Easy oven-cleaning.* Warm your oven; turn it off. Place a small bowl of ammonia inside. Close the door and let it sit overnight. Wipe clean in the morning.

311. *Even oven racks can shine.* Soak oven racks in a towel-lined tub with ammonia and hot water.

312. *Vacuum under your refrigerator regularly.* This is where you

find the fan and the condenser. You will also find pet hairs and dust balls.

313. *Empty the clothes dryer lint trap.* A full trap makes your dryer work harder.

314. *Clean out your toaster often.* Feed crumbs to the birds.

315. *Make your microwave sparkle.* Heat a cup of water for two or three minutes in the microwave. Let sit awhile. Wipe the microwave clean inside.

316. *Clean your hot water heater every year.*

317. *Keep an ABC fire extinguisher where you might need it.* Mine are in the kitchen (away from the stove) and in the bedroom, next to the flashlight. I recommend a #5 ABC extinguisher. "ABC" means the extinguisher is rated for all types of fires. "BC" is rated for electrical or grease and oil, but not for wood, paper, or anything solid. What is your house made of?

Remember to check your fire extinguisher gauge. Once a year, turn your extinguisher upside down and shake to loosen the chemical.

318. *Change your vacuum cleaner bags often!* Your vacuum may be a Super-cadillac-deluxe model, but it will work no better than its filtering system. You spend $1,000 on a vacuum because you really, really want to keep your carpets clean. Fran from my janitor supply store says you can probably do as good a job with the $200 model if you change your bags *a lot.* Think how many bags $800 could buy!

A vacuum cleaner will lose between 25 and 50 percent efficiency after only 1/4 cup of fine dust accumulates in the bag. If your bag is too full, your vacuum will grind heavy dirt into your floor. This dirt acts like tiny scissors and cuts the fiber of your carpet. Pet hair and dandruff rot in the bag in any humidity at all. Dust mites thrive in the dark, humid environment of your filter bag. When you turn on your machine, microscopic pores act like little doorways—baby dust mites explode into the room!

319. *Use double-density, anti-bacterial vacuum cleaner bags.* I do. They are more expensive than normal bags but I consider this important for my business—and for health in my home.
320. *Check the revolving brush roller on your vacuum cleaner.* Long hair and string are death to a vacuum.
321. *Regularly change the belt on your vacuum cleaner motor.*
322. *When buying a vacuum, check with the folks who repair them to find your best buy.* I bought an excellent commercial vacuum from Fran for one-third the price. It was an overhauled trade-in.
323. *Become attached to your vacuum attachments:* clean blinds, edge along walls, reach difficult spots, clean furniture.
324. *Vacuum often.* Your carpet will last much longer. Manufacturers suggest twice a week for normal traffic areas.
325. *Vacuum in two different directions—six times over a spot is recommended.* I'm not fooling.
326. *Keep the carpets warranty-worthy.* Most factory warranties for carpets require proof that they have been professionally cleaned every 18 months.
327. *Be careful with rental machines when shampooing carpet.* If you get the carpet too wet you might break down or dissolve the backing; too much detergent could leave a residue which attracts more soil!
328. *Use carpet "runners" and entrance mats.*
329. *Best entranceway:* a hard surface flooring where a mat greets your feet.
330. *Make a cheap and effective window cleaning solution.* Use one drop of dish soap in one quart of water.
331. *Wash windows with a soft, lint-free rag, using homemade window cleaner.* Or use plain water (trust me!). Do not wash in extreme heat or sunshine.
332. *Use a squeegee.* I recommend buying a professional squeegee where window washing equipment is sold, not from a discounter; they don't work as well. A good squeegee is invaluable and will save you time. An old broom handle will help you

reach higher windows. Yes, I learned to dry windows with newspapers, too—but now I use a squeegee.

- With the squeegee, make a two-inch border along the top of the washed window.
- Place the squeegee in the border area and pull down as far as you can go, without stopping.
- Wipe squeegee with damp rag after each pass.
- If you end up with water spots, you have hard-water stains. Use full-strength fabric softener and let sit on the glass awhile. Rinse well. Resist the temptation to spray outside windows with your hose unless you like hard water stains.

333. *Homemade cleaners?* Many people promote the use of common household supplies for cleaning. Although I advocate this approach, there are times when "homemade" does not work well. Or sometimes I'd rather roll up my sleeves to bat a ball than to work as hard as Grandma did. For when you want them, here are some useful ideas for "homemade":

- Furniture polish: Mix equal parts turpentine, vinegar and linseed oil.
- General cleaner: Mix equal parts ammonia and water in spray bottle. Use for appliances, counters, etc.
- Porcelain cleaner: paste of Borax and lemon juice.
- Chrome cleaner and carpet stain cleaner: straight vinegar.
- Drain cleaner: 1/2 box of baking soda, followed by a cup of vinegar. Once the "action" stops, run hot water down drain.

334. *Baking soda—use it for everything!* Ten sure-fire hints follow:

335. *Soak baby bottles, thermos bottles, etc. in baking soda and water.* Gets rid of the sour smell.

336. *Remove perspiration stains.* Make a paste of baking soda and water.

337. *Clean fiberglass.* Sprinkle baking soda on a wet sponge.

338. *Soak a smelly dishcloth in baking soda and water.*

339. *Soak burnt-on "goo" in pan bottoms with baking soda and water.*

340. *Sprinkle baking soda in kitty's litter box.* Helps deodorize it.

341. *Scrub away stains from coffee or tea.* Use baking soda on a wet sponge.

342. *Flush contents of an old box of baking soda down the kitchen sink (use lots of water) to keep pipes clean and fresh.*

343. *Clean—and deodorize—inside of fridge and freezer.* Wash with baking soda in water.

344. *Puppy accidents on the carpet: Sprinkle baking soda on the spot.* Vacuum when dry. It's a deodorizer for carpets.

345. *Bug off!* My friend Bob is an exterminator. I asked him how to keep bugs out of the house. He says:

- Do not keep firewood in or alongside your home. It is job security for Bob.
- Do not keep a dirty house; be careful with food, crumbs, garbage, scraps.
- Vacuum as often as you can, especially if you have animals.
- Bark or wood chip ground cover around the house is not sensible, according to Bob. Decaying material is an attraction for insects.
- Keep the foundation area of your home clean.
- Insect problems do not get better. If they are caught early, a barrier service outside will cost much less.

346. *Save hospitality for people, not ants.* When people see ants where do they put bait canisters? Inside the house. "Why would you want to attract bugs?" asks Bob.

347. *Use bug spray with caution; read the label.* It's lethal stuff.

348. *Do it yourself!* Simple home-mending chores are easily tackled. How-to books and videos are at the library. Need an inexpensive helper? Call the guidance counselor at the local high school and ask for a recommendation.

349. *Supplies to keep on hand:* hammer, Phillips and regular screw-

drivers, Yankee drill, pliers, assorted nails and screws, wood and glass glue.

350. *Rent tools you need for a project if you cannot borrow them.* Need a ladder for painting? Rent one. Need a power-wash for your home before you paint? Rent one. Need a paint sprayer? Rent one.

351. *Consider painting the outside of your own home.* If you paint your own home, you can save thousands of dollars. You must, however, get beyond the "icky paint stage," says my painter friend Dave. (I'm not fooling, that's what he said.) People hate to paint because paint drips, runs down their arms, and they do not know how to handle the materials. Learn technique. Borrow a book or a "how-to" video from the library. Do not be overwhelmed. Do a wall at a time. Prepare to get dirty.

352. *To protect against drips, use dropcloths.* These don't need to be those specially marketed "official" dropcloths; just cover the area with an old sheet or with plastic.

353. *Wash your siding really well first.* This makes all the difference in the world in helping the paint adhere. Rent a power-washer; use a stiff brush.

354. *Rent a paint sprayer.* Most paint stores rent equipment.

355. *Mask off windows or anything you do not want painted.* Use newspapers! If you use masking tape remove it pronto because it leaves a residue.

356. *Consider a better housepaint.* Most stores carry two qualities of paint. Professional painters always use the highest quality. Unless you want to paint your home again and again, inside or out, please consider a better paint. Cheaper in the long run.

357. *Look for paint with a higher proportion of acrylic solids.* Acrylic solids are what makes paint durable. Cheaper paints have more water, or filler, and less solids. Washability is an important consideration when buying paint: The more water in the paint, the less washable and the poorer the paint will perform on a "scrub test."

358. *Try to get that higher quality paint for a lower price.* Ask stores if they plan a sale on their better paint, if you can get a price break because of quantity purchase, or if they have returns they will sell for greatly reduced cost.

359. *Don't scrimp on priming.* Always prime if going over fresh wood or new construction.

360. *Buy a good brush.* It will help you to do a good job with little dripping. A good brush will cost much more but will last a lifetime. Look for high-quality, soft bristles that are longer. Cheap brushes are stiff, lose their bristles in your paint, and hold less paint.

361. *Ask for additives to retard drying and help paint flow.* Paint stores sell them. Ever try to paint a door? Know how it comes out streaky, with brush marks? Know why professional painters get doors to come out smooth and even? Those additives.

362. *Ask for other additives for special needs.* Products are available that block old smoke smell, grease, mildew formation, and stains.

363. *Buy the right paint for the job. Know your paint types:* 1. Flat: This is the least washable, although higher quality will be somewhat washable. It has no sheen and is the least durable. Flat paint has the nicest aesthetic appeal because it is the most pleasing and soft. 2. Velvet: Washable; looks almost flat; has greater longevity. Velvet or flat looks good on rough-cut wood. 3. Eggshell: Intermediate stage between velvet and semigloss. 4. Semigloss: Shinier; good in kitchen, bath or laundry; has more body; washable, durable. 5. High gloss: Shiniest; most durable and washable. Classic looks are nice with shinier trim. Shiny lasts longer.

364. *Freeze-frame your paint job!* Tired of painting for the day? Put your brush in a sturdy plastic bag and into the freezer. The freezer?! Yep. I do this all the time. Saves daily clean-up. Defrost for 30 minutes. I once did this for an entire summer.

365. *Achieve fancy effects with paint.* False ("faux") finish is simply painting a surface to make it look like a different surface. If you want an old look, or a marble look, you might be able to create a false finish with paint. Here is what we did:

I recently ripped carpet squares off our kitchen floor. Without carpet I was down to the original cabin floor, tongue and groove... and badly worn. I loved it! But the floor needed more structural stability. We achieved it with painted plywood. Joe borrowed an iron straight-edge to cut shallow lines lengthwise, giving the illusion of individual boards. I wanted an old, worn, persimmon kind of color and practiced with stain until I had the effect. I used an artist's brush to apply black paint down each groove. With three layers of clear acrylic finish and a couple of throw rugs (thrift store), I had a new old-fashioned floor! For under $100! It tied in visually with our calico-lined open shelves and gave my small kitchen a dynamite decorator look.

366. *Landscape it yourself too!* Now that you've painted your home, what about the moonscape you are living on? Time to fix, but no money, right? Maybe these tips will help:

367. *Neat and tidy doesn't cost a thing.*

368. *Sit outside and draw landscape plans on paper.* Do you have natural features? Highlight them! Figure out how you can spruce things up.

369. *Take advantage of free landscaping advice.* Some garden centers offer landscaping advice. Ask if there is a fee. Some fees are refunded with the purchase of merchandise.

370. *Consider "found" items:* rocks, driftwood, etc.

371. *Look for used brick at construction sites.* Can you make a walkway or interesting planter treatment?

372. *Ask friends or family for cuttings of perennials or bushes.* A friend gave me ivy clippings. Now one of the prettiest spots outside our home is an ivy bed made from a recycled railroad tie and a piece of old painted trellis. It ties together a big fir tree and rock

on one end with a natural bank on the other. The ivy has filled this two-foot-wide bed and is climbing the fir and trellis. I planted violas in the midst of this rich-looking display. Even Grim grins. Cost to us? About $2 for the flowers, which, as perennials, come back each year.

373. *Buy lesser quality sod from sod farms, if they have it.* Grows just as well.

374. *Need dirt?* Maybe a neighbor will share the cost of a load.

375. *Plant a few trees and bushes first,* before you worry about flowers to line your walk. They are a better investment.

376. *Do some research before planting trees.* Joseph knows trees. He oversees the planting of baby trees in this area of Montana. He cautions you not to transplant trees in the summer. The heat is tough on a tree, which will use all its energy just to survive. The best time to transplant trees and shrubs is early spring and fall.

377. *Consider the future maintenance of new trees.* Do not create a project that requires lots of future maintenance. I had the romantic notion of planting a new tree each year. Being the practical type, I wanted to plant fruit-bearing trees. Nice idea, but keep something in mind: Fruit trees require maintenance and spraying. Some require pollination. So much for romance.

378. *Prune your own trees.* Rent equipment when necessary.

379. Last but not least, *Do NOT include landscaping costs in your mortgage.* You will pay dearly for those trees and bushes for the next 25 years! And you will regret it!

EIGHT

Put Pizzazz in Your Palace

Our home is small. And it is not fancy. Yet we welcome people through in shifts! Does our house shout "We're glad you're here"? You bet it does! It even shouts, "Howdy, partner, pull up a chair and set a spell!" Have we pumped a lot of money into getting it this way? Absolutely not.

If you are discouraged because decorating dollars don't even qualify for a slot on your budget, then buck up, Buckaroo! This chapter is for you!

Bookshelves out of pork and beans. My sister Anne loves pork and beans. She always has a can or two in her pantry. Anne said it all one day: "Hey, if worse comes to worst I can make bookshelves out of cans of pork and beans!"

Anne has the right attitude. Remember the commandments on attitude and creativity? If things go poorly for her and she has no money to make her home pretty, she can always use what she has. So can you!

Anne likes a Southwestern motif and has collected lots of Mexican ware to accent her home. Joe and I have rustic furniture. We live in a cabin on a lake. It would be silly for me to turn my home into art deco. Take another look at your house. What do you have that you can build around? What can you dust off or haul out of storage to put pizzazz in your palace?

This little piggy... After Mama died, Joe and I selected special possessions from her home. One was a clay piggy bank. The rosy-cheeked critter came home with us. Where did we put the pig? In the bathroom! We wrote "Thank Offering" across the back of the bank and stuck a note on top: "All money placed in here goes to feed the hungry—in Jesus' name."

Piggy is emptied a few times each year and an astonishing amount of money falls out. Where did it come from? From people who have recognized the meaning of their gift in the privacy and silence of that room. They have reached willingly into their pockets to share, without notice, without acknowledgement, and without appreciation. And that is the greatest kind of giving. Piggy stands smiling up at everyone with thanks.

Moral of the story? Look at what you have in a new way. Even a pig in the bathroom can glorify the Lord!

Calico can too! Okay, maybe you like doors on cabinets. I don't! And that's good for us. When we remodeled this old camp we joked about our "Post-Modern Garage Sale" approach. We cut corners where we could. Rather than face each predicament with "cannot" we developed a "can too" with calico.

By using fabric we were able to create a charming rustic, country feel to our home at a fraction of the cost of ordinary cabinets, curtains, pillows, closet doors. We have used strips of calico to accent old curtains and pull a room together. We have curtained off otherwise doorless closets. We have covered an entire shelving unit by gluing calico on the top and bottom of each shelf. This is the open shelf on which I keep my dishes. Is there an application for fabric in your home? Find a pattern you like and drape it over a shower curtain or cabinet door to get a "feel" for how it looks. You might decide that you can calico, too!

"Dear Carol... Help!" I wrote to our interior designer friend. "I need some cheap tips on how to decorate a house!" I also talked with Tedi, a friend who "does windows." Here are their hints, along with some of my own:

$uper $avers

380. *Look at what you have in a new way.* Use available resources found in the attic, basement, or garden.
381. *Paint is the quickest, cheapest way to make a major change.* (See previous chapter.)
382. *Change color of trim,* inside or out.
383. *Stencil a border* at ceiling or chair rail height.
384. Run a *wallpaper border* at ceiling or chair rail height. Look for odd, leftover rolls of border; buy on sale.
385. *Nail a decorative board horizontally,* at chair rail height.
386. *Rearrange existing furniture.*
387. *Move hanging pictures to new locations.*
388. *Reduce "clutter" on countertops and tables.*
389. *Make napkins or runners* and give tabletops a fresh look. Search scrap bins at fabric stores.
390. *Arrange bouquets of fresh-cut flowers.*
391. *Decorate with plants* in all types of containers.
392. *Make new curtains to match existing fabric* on chairs, sofas, comforters, etc.
393. *Make your own drapes,* if you possess the time and talent; and if you can find the fabric on sale. Draperies are expensive but are needed in some situations like insulating patio doors. They also create a more formal look. If you don't sew, there are other ways to find some suitable used drapes.
394. *Check for drapery trade-ins.* Ask stores that make drapes if they are getting trades or have any used drapes on hand.
395. *Use the want ads.* Put in an ad for the more expensive items you need, such as drapes.
396. *Check thrift stores.* (I see drapes often.)
397. *Take care of your drapes.* Dry cleaning is hard on drapes. There is

a new service, however, that professionally dry cleans drapes at your home. It's easier on the drapes and eliminates taking them down.

398. *Consider mini-blinds or pleated, honeycomb, or vertical shades* if you have a difficult window to cover. You will need to balance the extra cost by saving money elsewhere.

399. *Stay neutral.* If you invest in blinds or shades opt for a neutral or conservative color. This eliminates conflict if you change color schemes later. Add color on top with a valance or cornice board, etc.

400. *Drape doilies or cloth napkins over a brass rod* for a quick and cute valance treatment for a window. Experiment.

401. *Fewer cabinets, more baskets!* Use hanging baskets in the bathroom to collect toiletries, hair-care products, pretty sponges, a collection of soaps.

402. *Inexpensive storage:* Use hanging baskets in the kitchen. I have one two-tier basket for all big spoons and spatulas; and one three-tier basket for onions and garlic, the top basket filled with cookie cutters.

403. *Make a patchwork rug for a small room* using coordinated carpet-sample squares.

404. *Create a seasonal bouquet.* Pick a few bare branches in the fall, pine boughs in winter, wildflowers in the spring, and flowers in summer. Find a spot in your home that will catch the eye, so your "special bouquet" will greet everyone.

405. *Make flowers last longer.* Flowers keep fresher if put in the refrigerator overnight.

406. *Buy inexpensive "greens" instead of expensive-cut flowers* from your florist. Highlight them with a silk flower or ribbon.

407. *Table treatment:* Scatter straw flowers, colored leaves, and small gourds all over your table when entertaining in the fall. Do the same with small pine boughs or holly in the winter, flowers in the spring. I do this to rave reviews!

408. *Art on a shoestring.* Frame a high quality greeting card, calendar page or magazine picture.

409. *Hang a colorful birdhouse in your kitchen.* I did!

410. *Brighten the corner where you are.* Yellow harmonizes with many colors and adds brightness and warmth to a room.

411. *Decorate with your collector's items.* Kristin collects interesting plates and platters from garage sales and thrift stores. She hangs them in the bathroom: steam resistant.

412. *Entertain with your collection!* Buy odds and ends of dishes in color combinations such as blue and white, black and gold, florals. Makes spectacular table settings!

413. *Light for a dramatic setting:* If you're not using your fireplace, put an assortment of candles inside.

414. *Jazz up the plain stuff.* Stencil a design on a small wooden nightstand.

415. *Lighten up!* Change to a crisper, lighter color on your walls or cabinets.

416. *Change the hardware on your cabinets.*

417. *Paint appliances a new color.* If nervous doing it yourself, ask an auto body shop for a bid. Caution: Consider the overall condition of the appliance before you invest in a new color.

418. *Change lampshades.*

419. *Set the base of your lamp inside a colorful basket.*

420. *Make throw pillows.* Make throw pillows by stuffing two matching washcloths or handtowels sewn together. I have a pillow that is twenty-four years old and still going strong. I toss it in the wash a couple times a year.

421. *Staple fabric on a headboard* to create a new look in a bedroom.

422. *Don't buy fancy play equipment.* Create a desk or fort for your child by cutting down an old appliance box. Let the child decorate with markers, stickers, paint.

Sheets, sheets, sheets! Instead of buying expensive yard goods, buy sheets. They come in a variety of colors and prints. Use them for all sorts of interior decorating applications:

423. *Tablecloth, runners, napkins*—all can be sewn from sheets, even old ones.

424. *Curtains, valances, curtain liners, comforters*—more sheets.

425. *Blanket saver.* Sew two sheets together and stick a blanket inside. Looks nice. Keeps blanket clean—fewer dry cleaning bills!

426. *Reupholster a chair with sheets.*

427. *Make a decorative shower curtain cover out of a bright sheet.* People will never guess that it used to be a sheet.

428. *Crazy sheets.* Kristin not only does wonders with dishes, she buys plain white or cream top sheets (on sale, odds and ends) and the WILDEST bottom (fitted) sheets she can find!

429. *Make a "hammock" for stuffed toys* using an old sheet: Fold into a triangle, tack one end in a corner, other ends on the wall.

430. *Line the back seat of your car with a sheet* (dog protection).

431. *Make a children's fort by draping a sheet over a card table* (if you're out of appliance boxes!)

432. *Inexpensive pillow cases*—make new ones out of the parts of a sheet that aren't as worn.

433. *Use old sheets as drop cloths.* Don't buy anything for that job!

434. *Cut up sheets and use as fabric for miscellaneous sewing.*

FURNITURE

"You pay for an inferior product twice—once when you buy it and again when you pay to replace it before its time." That is an old carpenter's proverb. Sadly, for most of us, that is also a fact of life. This book has consistently recommended that you buy quality, take care of it, and it will last. That is not always possible. Yet a little knowledge may help you avoid costly mistakes.

I admit it—I came to the subject of furniture with a strong bias against buying new, based exclusively on my distaste for furniture-selling ads. ("Crafty sales pitch" is more like it!) I am annoyed and perplexed by sales offers: no money down, no interest, no payment until you are 529 years old! "Gimmick!" I yell at the TV. In retail you get what you pay for, and when you sign up for neat-sounding deals you are usually paying enough interest to choke a full-grown Clydesdale! OR their inflated prices more than compensate for their "low" interest.

But I do buy furniture from time to time, sometimes new, often used. How do I make good decisions?

Essentially, most furniture can be graded good, better, and best. It is up to you to know the difference. Ask questions. Consider the environment the furniture will be moved to: Do you have youngsters, pets, young adults (of the floppy variety)? Humid or dry climate? Less expensive furniture is usually made with a soft wood, such as pine. Better furniture comes with a hardwood frame. Best furniture is made from hardwood that is kiln dried. How well will soft wood hold up in your home? You must consider these things before you commit yourself to a major purchase.

Antiques. "Antique" does not necessarily mean chairs with spindly legs that collapse if someone actually sits on them! Antiques can be pretty rugged. There is much to say about a piece of furniture that is made from good solid wood. In our home we have (through inheritance) an antique oak bed and four oak dressers that are going to be around long after we are gone. They are sturdy, beautiful—and valuable. Most non-antique furniture, no matter the quality, depreciates faster than a speeding nightstand! A well-preserved antique can appreciate in value.

Get real! This book is about *frugal* living! You may object, "It's not exactly frugal to buy expensive furnishings!" You're right! But it is frugal to know where to spot good furniture, right? Don't pay full price for anything; get the good stuff as cheaply as possible and use it forever.

435. *How do you spot a good piece of furniture?* Let's consider a couch:

- Coil springs should go all the way to the edge of the seat (under where cushions go). Is the couch board-hard on the edge? Lower quality.
- Upholstery material should go all the way to the back on the bottom (under where cushions go). Does the couch only have a few inches of upholstery and then a different fabric? Lower quality.
- You should be able to turn pillows over and use both sides. If not, or if there's no cushion at all, it's lower quality.
- Cushions should be heavy. If you can easily pick up a seat cushion with one hand you do not have a quality piece of furniture.
- Frames should be hardwood for better quality. Softwood means lower quality. Pine, for instance, is a soft wood; oak is hard. Always ask if the piece is hardwood.
- Plates that support legs should be big. Loose legs? Lower quality.

Now, armed with your quality indicators, let's talk about where to look for good furniture, and special tricks you can employ with what you find.

$uper $avers

436. *Look for nice, used furniture or sturdy, useful antiques.*

437. *Check the basements of furniture stores,* where you can find mismatched, orphaned pieces, or trade-ins.

438. *Keep alert for garage sales, moving sales.*

439. *Remember auctions, estate sales.*

440. *Newspaper (classified) ads* often feature good furniture.

441. *Consider buying secondhand furniture if you have young children.* When they are grown, replace it.

442. *Buy something that is dual-purpose:* a sofa-bed, an old "decorator trunk" for storage. (Joe's favorite footrest is extra storage for sugar and flour.)

443. *Use paint to revive your finds.* Paint works miracles on old footstools, magazine racks, end tables. Paint the legs of your wooden table white; leave the tabletop natural wood.

444. *Re-cover the seats of your kitchen or dining room chairs.* It's easy to do on some chairs. I have done this in minutes using matching towels or—what else?—calico.

445. *Make your own nightstand.* Put a round piece of wood on top of any kind of base (we use two cardboard open-faced "filing cabinets"). Cover with small tablecloth. For added drama, we covered the top of our tablecloth with a shawl.

446. *Check office supply stores* for clearance items.

447. *Buy unfinished furniture* and paint or stain it yourself.

448. *Use slipcovers.* A few slipcovers and a new accent rug can complement a different paint color and give your home zip! Can't afford slipcovers? Oh, yes, you can (see page 118).

449. *Re-upholster your tired furniture.* On average, reupholstering costs 60 percent of what it costs to buy the same piece of quality furniture new. There are times when reupholstering a piece is sensible, when you have furniture of high workmanship or sentiment, for example.

450. *Find a reputable upholsterer and ask if there is any way you can cut costs without affecting the result.* Does he or she have material on hand? Can the job be limited to only part of the piece? Can you supply the fabric?

Do-It-Yourself Slipcovers

Assemble safety pins, drapery pins, a tape measure, a yardstick, and scissors.

- Measure. Figure how much fabric you need. Begin all measurements at floor level. (a) Measure up the arms, over the back, down the other arm. Add a yard to your total and you have the width. (b) Measure from the front, up over the seat, up the back, down the back. Add a yard to your total and you have the length. Measure each cushion in both directions and add three inches to each measurement. Rule of thumb: A chair generally requires six to nine yards of material. A sofa, twelve to eighteen yards. Once you have the measurements, buy a flat sheet to fit the frame, and another to cover the cushions.
- Take cushions off chair; center the sheet.
- Smooth the sheet everywhere. Tuck the fabric *well* using the yardstick. Cut off excess material at floor level, trying to make round corners.
- Use pins to pleat sheet around chair arms. You may even want to use a staple gun to attach the material to the wood frame. If you cannot hide the pins, don't worry; just make cover-up "ties" when you are finished.
- Wrap each cushion, pinning the material together on the bottom of the cushion with safety pins.
- Use extra material to make strips to glue or tie around perimeter, or use ribbon or cording.

CARPETS

If you are looking for the least expensive floor covering in America today, consider carpet. This means relying on a knowledgeable person at a reputable store to ensure the most for your money.

Gerry from the carpet store tells me that on the average, floor covering is purchased every seven to ten years. There are many sensational-sounding offers as stores compete for your money. How do you sift through the promotion and get to the bottom line: good carpet, good price? Is there any carpet lingo that will help you find a fix for your floor?

According to Gerry, there is no industry-wide standard for rating carpet. Standardized ratings may come soon. A few carpets do have ratings. Learn them and you will have enough savvy to do business. Until full-disclosure selling is universal you will have to ask, ask, ask! When shopping for carpet, consider fiber type, durability, "twist rate," and weight before you consider color and type of weave.

Fiber. There are the following general types of fiber, each manufactured with different blends:

- Nylon: most resilient, cleans well, can fade.
- Olefin: most naturally stain resistant, resists fading, least resilient.
- Polyester: most vivid colors, resists fading, will pill and fuzz.
- Natural fibers: wool, some cotton. Makes up less than 3 percent of the market. Has the softest feel; it is also the most difficult to clean.

Durability. Durability is tested by trafficking the equivalent of 20,000 people over a carpet. "Test people" are stopped every fifteen minutes and the carpet vacuumed. At each interval a brand new piece of that carpet is held in comparison. This test is designed to simulate the normal use of five to ten years. If ratings are applied:

1 to 1-1/2	=	light traffic
2-1/2 to 4	=	normal traffic
4 to 5	=	heavy traffic

Twist rate. Twist rate determines how much "memory" a carpet has, and how well it will bounce back. If ratings are applied:

5, 6, 7	=	very good
4 to 5	=	good
below 3	=	minimal

Weight. Weight is the number of ounces of face-fiber per square yard. When considering weight, be certain you are getting carpet weight per square yard that does not include backing or pads. A good rule of thumb: Carpets that have a face weight of 35 ounces or more per square yard are generally good quality.

Whew! Did you know all that? I didn't! I always bought what looked nice and was affordable. And you know what? I have one room in this house with horrid carpeting! Oh, I thought I was cutting a fine deal! "Base grade," it was called. "Base" means "poor in quality." It was all we could afford back then. But it looks awful now. I would have done better to have painted my floor and added throw rugs! Gerry said his biggest tip is to buy something that will hold up. I second that with a hearty "Amen!"

Read on for more tips on carpet buying:

$uper $avers

451. *Direct from the mill?* Advertisements read, "Save up to 50 percent! Buy direct!" This can be money-saving, but you must be wise and consider all expenses. Before you order, be sure to check:
    - Cost of installation
    - Cost of freight
    - Cost of pads
    - Cost of exact same carpet from local merchant
    - What happens if carpet is flawed

452. *Try a used-carpet franchise.* In some parts of the country a used-carpet franchise is becoming popular. This would be a great place to begin your search.

453. *Talk with a local merchant.* Ask him to keep you in mind if he comes across good used carpet. Tell him your needs and wants, then patiently wait to see what he encounters.

454. *Remnant packages.* Many carpet stores order remnant packages and can offer higher quality for less price. Some remnants won't be large enough for your whole house. You might run one color though the common area of your home and different colors in bedrooms.

455. *Watch newspaper ads for used carpet.*

456. *Take advantage of year-end sales.* There are no seasonal sales in carpets, but a genuine end-of-year inventory sale is a good opportunity for the consumer. The merchant wants merchandise to go!

457. *This is a big decision! Do you need help?* Consider a store that has an interior design consultant to help make your decision.

458. *Take your time when choosing color and style.*

459. *Check out your installer's credentials.* Does the installer carry "completed operations" liability insurance? He should. Insurance is a sign that you are probably dealing with an experienced professional. Regrettably, inexperienced people often advertise services for which they do not have training.

460. *Try to purchase a good pad.* This takes stress off carpet. A good pad could make it possible for you to buy a lesser quality carpet.

461. *Extend the life of your carpet.* Provide an adequate hard-surface walk-off area with a mat to wipe your feet at the door. Use runners in traffic areas.

462. *Buy the best value you can afford.*

463. *If you can't afford good enough carpeting, "buy time":* (I didn't say "buy *on* time"!) If I had to temporarily cover a floor until I could afford carpeting, I would paint the floor or search thrift stores until I found an area rug. I would then learn everything I could about carpets and develop a good rapport with a dealer. That person would know my earnest need and would think of

me the split second an excellent used carpet or a really good remnant or close-out came along. That's what I'd do.

APPLIANCES

Dean has been fixing appliances for a long time, so I went to him. If you want to know how a particular product or brand performs, ask the fellow or gal who does repairs; and be prepared to take counsel.

You can save a bundle if you purchase appliances used. You can also waste money and buy someone's headache. This section will give advice on what to look for in a used appliance. Some of us "bite the bullet" and purchase new. If you do, be alert to price, quality, and energy efficiency. Keep in mind that the cheapest advertised appliance may be just that: cheap in quality and efficiency. It may also be a "loss leader" to get you in the showroom door. Do your homework: Shop around, ask questions, check magazines, and chat with friends. Look for a store that will guarantee lowest price.

Average Life Expectancy of Major Appliances

(According to Dean)

Refrigerator	10 to 12 years
Freezer	14 to 16 years
Stove	16 to 18 years
Washing machine	12 to 14 years
Dryer	16 to 18 years
Hot water heater	20 to 25 years
Microwave	8 to 10 years
Dishwasher	10 to 12 years

$uper $avers

464. *A few questions to consider if buying from a major discounter:* Who will install your appliance? Who will train you in its use? Who will service it if something goes wrong?

465. *Learn how to use your appliance!* It comes with an "instruction manual." We are supposed to READ our manual and learn proper operation. Grim reminds me regularly of a few buttons on my washer and drier that I have yet to figure out!

466. *If buying a used refrigerator or freezer,* look for cracks in the liner and rubber all around the opening. This sort of thing spreads like cancer. A bad seal causes the appliance to work hard and wastes electricity.

467. *Also look at the back of the fridge. See if a "tap" has been attached to the compressor.* If the valve mechanism has been tapped it was serviced and life expectancy is short.

468. *Ask if the compressor has been changed.* If so, how long ago? You will get five or six years more service from a new compressor.

469. *Check for odors.* Many go away once the refrigerator is cooled.

470. *Look for refrigerators with top or bottom freezers.* They have greater efficiency than side-mounted freezers.

471. *Keep your refrigerator seal clean.* Wash regularly.

472. *A chest freezer has greater efficiency than an upright,* but is less convenient to use.

473. *If shopping for a used stove,* make sure the oven door gasket is sound and seals well. Ditto hinges.

474. *Check the stove temperatures for accuracy.* Use an oven thermometer. Note: All older electric stoves can be subject to a "50 degree throw." If temperature is set at 300°F, the temperature can go up to 325°F and shut off; then down to 275°F and go back on. Some new stoves will do this as well, although most have sensors that keep temperature within five to ten degrees.

475. *Don't expect the clock to work on a used stove.* Most replacement clocks cost more than a used stove.

476. *Self-cleaners are a good buy because of great oven insulation,* which is especially appreciated during summer use.

477. *If you buy a gas stove or dryer, ask the gas company to check installation for leaks.* This service is free.

478. *Do not put aluminum foil under your electric oven elements!* Foil reflects heat back onto the element and cuts life in half. It also "lies" to the thermostat.

479. *When buying a used washing machine, check for rust* on the lid and in the tub.

480. *Also check hoses for cracks and weaknesses.*

481. *Straight agitator fins do not wash as efficiently* as wavy fins, or "splines," which tumble clothes.

482. *Be certain to match washer and dryer in size*—a dryer should not be smaller than the wash load.

483. *Stick with a dryer that operates on 220 volts,* rather than 110.

484. *Never buy a used hot water heater*—too much chance for a rusted or clogged unit.

485. *When buying a new water heater, look for a four-inch clean-out valve.* If you drain it every two years you will clear out calcium and iron and the elements will last longer.

486. *Put an insulating blanket around your water heater.* You may get a credit from your utility company. Check with the manufacturer first, though, since some insulation applications are not advisable.

487. *Most microwaves should be bought new.* There may be a good used buy if you watch ads, but know what you are getting.

488. *Do not open the microwave while it is running.* Turn it off first. Otherwise you will burn out your switches.

489. *Make sure you have no chips in the liner of your microwave.* You don't want a microwave that leaks radiation!

490. *Keep the glass of your microwave clear of grease and dirt.* Dirty microwaves interfere with peak performance.

491. *The Big Bang Theory of Microwave Disorders.* This is going to throw you for a loop; it did me. It's about microwave popcorn. Dean thinks that cooking popcorn in your microwave will cut it down in the prime of its life! Dean admits it is only a theory, but he has repaired many a microwave that has been used extensively for popcorn popping. Anyway, we discussed the bad economy of buying that stuff in the food chapter.

492. *Don't buy a used dishwasher unless it's under a year old.*

493. *There is a 50/50 chance you will do well with a used portable dishwasher.*

494. *Check gaskets* when buying a used dishwasher.

495. *Look for a three-level wash feature* when buying a dishwasher. It's the most efficient.

496. *Use dry dishwasher detergent.* I'm told that liquid dishwasher soap does not break down. It gums everything up after a while. Yuck.

497. *If buying a used appliance from a dealer, ask if you are entitled to a 30- or 90-day warranty,* no matter what type of used appliance you purchase.

NINE

Money Talk: Control the Credit Crunch

A wise old saying taped to our mirror reads: "He who lives content with little possesses everything." Are you content? Or are you never satisfied? Are you on a treadmill to get more things, or at peace with whatever you have? Do you make loan installments, car payments, boat payments? Do bills come your way each month from credit card companies for furniture purchases, VCRs, trips, cameras, campers, sports equipment, outings, musical tapes, books...? Whew! Need I go on?

Live within your means. Some people have no choice but to live within their means. We call them poor. Poor people! We speak as if being poor is a threat, a bad thing, something to be avoided at all cost!... At all cost.

Isn't living within your means what this book is all about? Grim yells "No! Live BELOW your means!" He has a point. Does your family live within its means? If there is more "outgo" than income each month you are in trouble. How do you get out of trouble? Look it squarely in the eye.

Prepare for shock. Once we determined to be content with little, Joe and I began to analyze our circumstances, and that was the beginning of our climb from the slippery money pit. If you want to live within your means, you must honestly evaluate how you manage money.

This chapter is designed to give you a gentle push, a bit of encouragement, and some friendly advice to help you handle finances more efficiently. Two important comments: (1) The Bible tells us the love of money is the root of many evils. Please do not become obsessive in money management; do not become a slave to this master. You have one Master; you cannot possibly serve two. (2) A friend named Paula gave me advice twenty years ago. Her words stick like glue! Paula said when I fail I must pick myself up, dust myself off, and start again. Paula was right. Rather than despair when goals are not reached, I dust off my determination and start again. You can too!

Where does your money go? Sit down and determine exactly where your money goes. Be honest. And be prepared for surprise. This is your first step, and it is a big one.

Remember the commandment on organization? Track where your money goes. For instance, do you know how much of your pay goes for groceries? (According to the United States Department of Agriculture, the 1992 cost of food for a family of four was $460.80 a month—on a low-cost plan.) How much of your money goes for gasoline, for day care, for video rental? How much goes for installment payments or interest?

Take interest in your interest. How much of your hard-earned money goes toward interest payments? Few of us have any idea when we make those monthly payments. Do you really think minimum monthly payments are calculated for you to pay off your debt fast?! No way! Think you are striking a bargain when you buy a $1,000 mountain bike for $20 a month? It will cost nearly $2,000 and take ten years to pay off if you make minimum payments!

Are you paying as much as 25 percent more for your car because of interest? Are you stuck with unpaid balances on credit cards? Get interested in your affairs! If you do, you will be motivated to slash interest spending and live within your means.

My two cents. Know what I think? If most of us found the intestinal fortitude to examine our circumstances—bills, interest, mortgage, etc.—we would be shattered by the evidence. Few of us have considered living within our means.

It's scary to face such a predicament. Credit counselors tell me that some people—good people—are so frightened by their financial mess that they stop coping. Has that happened to you? Dust yourself off and find comfort that you are finally taking charge of your situation. Pray to the Father. Ask forgiveness if past mismanagement was from greed, covetousness, or selfishness. Ask for His help. ***He knows your heart.*** Crawl into His arms and say, "Dearest Father, I'm frightened about my money situation and I do not want it to consume me or take my attention off You, but I need Your help." Will He help you? You bet He will.

YOU NEED A BUDGET

There are two things we resolve to do on January 1: budget and diet. Am I wrong? Joe can vouch for my annual declaration: "That's it! No more spending! We're going to be in the poorhouse if we keep this up! We need a ***budget***, Joseph, and we ***need one now!*** And by the way, it's vegies and water from today forward! Happy New Year."

Budgeting rules. The Consumer Credit Counseling Service has compiled a list of eight helpful rules:

- Set realistic financial goals for yourself.
- Distinguish between wants and needs.
- Record monthly expenses to develop a realistic spending plan.
- Establish a savings plan.
- Limit monthly debt payments to 20 percent of net income (excluding mortgage).
- Build savings to include an emergency reserve of at least three months' income.
- Keep accurate records.
- Shop wisely.

You have taken a big step if you have faced your circumstances and have organized your financial situation. To write things down makes everything more tangible and more possible to put into perspective. Your next step is a budget, which can be a series of "baby steps." Go slowly. And be prepared to dust yourself off! What does it boil down to? *Live within your means!!*

Here are some budget tips to add to the above rules:

498. *The Consumer Credit Counseling Service offers worksheets* for people who want to establish financial accountability. Their budgets list monthly and non-monthly (or unexpected) expenses. The objective is to get expenses and income to balance. A phone call to this not-for-profit organization might set you on course (800-388-CCCS).

499. *A toll-free call to Christian Financial Concepts could be one of the smartest things you do.* Larry Burkett has been offering sound financial advice through seminars, books, and radio for years. His organization is dedicated to helping you gain control of finances while maintaining biblical fidelity. The address is P.O. Box 100, Gainesville, GA 30503 (phone: 800-722-1976).

500. *Bookstores sell workbooks* that help you work through your organizational maze.

501. *Free seminars* are offered by church, community, or government agencies.

502. *One system combines cash envelopes with your bank accounts.* Leslie budgets this way: She puts cash in separate envelopes: tithe, groceries, entertainment, miscellaneous (might include entertainment, haircuts, book purchases, stamps, etc.) She puts money needed for monthly bills into her checking account, and money for estimated taxes, quarterly insurance payments, etc. into savings.

503. *There is no one magic budget.* Budgets can be varied, creative, and tailor-made to fit your situation. Help in establishing a budget is not hard to find. Motivation is up to you.

BANKING

"There are bazillions of different types of loans and loan rates...." I was pretty impressed with a banker who talked about "bazillions," and sat forward to hear what Muffie had to say. In our town, Muffie has a sterling reputation—she would be the one to interview for this book. "Consumers are used to vanilla," she continued. "They say, 'I want a 30-year mortgage.' When possible, people are *tons* better off with a 15-year plan!" This had all the makings of a productive meeting.

Here's some of Muffie's banking expertise, packaged as advice to you:

504. *You need to know about the Standard Lender's Formula* that lending institutions use when considering a loan request:
   - Your house payment should be less than 28 percent of your gross income.
   - All of your debt, including house payment, should be less than 40 percent of your gross income.
   - Fifteen percent of your gross income should go to incidentals.
   - Twenty percent should be allowed for emergencies, entertainment, medical expenses, savings, etc.
   - A whopping $75 monthly is allowed for food for each adult; $50 per child. (Have they read national averages lately?! Muffie admits it's ridiculous.) The rest they presume to be absorbed by taxes.

   Would you qualify for a loan right now?

505. *Does the loan have origination or processing fees?* These are set-up fees for processing paperwork, etc. If you need a short-term loan, the addition of a processing fee might make even a low-interest loan a bad choice!

506. *Do not be afraid to ask questions.* Ask lenders how long they have been in business, if they have an interest rate-lock policy, and if you can get a lower rate.

507. *Ask how long it will take your lender to process your loan.*

508. *Remember that you can get loans structured to your needs.*

509. *Avoid unexpected costs.* Be absolutely certain you know what your total up-front or closing costs will be. No surprises.

510. *Consider timing when making arrangements for loan repayment.* Timing? Yep. Muffie will pay off the mortgage one year before her daughter heads to college.

511. *When possible, get an advance-type note that accrues interest only on the portion drawn.* Suppose you are remodeling your home and need $10,000 overall, but only $2,000 initially. Take out only what you need to avoid interest payments on the full amount of loan from the start.

512. *Read all terms and conditions.* Try to avoid penalty for prepayment of any loan you have.

513. *Think twice before you prematurely cash a certificate of deposit!* It may be wiser to take a short loan while your CD matures. The loan interest is usually cheaper than the penalty. Often there are no fees associated with CD-secured loans.

514. *Banks may offer a reduced rate on your consumer loan* if you have a special account OR if you have the fixed monthly payment automatically debited from your account.

515. *When shopping for a mortgage, review the Good Faith Estimate of Settlement Charges* (which must be supplied you). Is interest low, but are fees high? Are points separate from inspection fees?

516. *Pay attention to closing costs.* Some closing costs on a mortgage are tax-deductible. If you don't pay the fees separately, you will include them in your monthly payment and spread your deduction over the life of your mortgage. Would you rather have a one-time large deduction?

517. *Credit life insurance is generally a poor deal, as is disability coverage.* It's better to buy life or health insurance from another source. One exception is if you are in a high-risk occupation (e.g., logger, steelworker): Your occupation will not affect the

rate as it will with other insurance.

518. *Want to establish outstanding credit at a young age?* Pay off your student loan in a timely manner. Lenders will regard you as A-1, Super Duper, Best-All-Around Gal in the Country!

519. *Order the least expensive checks,* says Muffie, unless you are truly determined to have Elvis or pretty scenery staring up at you every time you pay the light bill! Some stationery and office supply firms sell checks. Many have introductory offers for checks at a significantly reduced cost compared to banks. Checks from a non-traditional check company generally cost less than half. Be certain to order three weeks before you need them.

520. *Cheapest checks of all.* Your bank might offer a package program that provides checks free. Ask.

521. *When to consider mortgage refinancing.* An interest differential greater than two percent may warrant a look at refinancing.

522. *If you lower your payment through refinancing, continue to pay the original amount.* You will retire your mortgage earlier than planned—at a possible savings of thousands!

523. *On the other hand . . .* If you reduce your mortgage interest load you will have less to deduct at tax time!

524. *Ask yourself these questions as you consider refinancing:* (provided by the Consumer Mortgage Information Bureau)
   - How long do you plan to live in your home?
   - What is the difference in interest between your current rate and the new rate?
   - What will it cost you to refinance?
   - Should you consider just switching to a different type of mortgage (i.e., variable rate or shorter duration)?

525. *To avoid bank penalties for bounced checks,* ask for a Ready Reserve Line of Credit. Nearly everyone qualifies for a credit line of $100; some people qualify for much more. Here is how it works: If you overdraw your account, the bank automatically

"loans" you an amount up to your credit line. Interest on this loan begins immediately, and the bank alerts you so you can make immediate restitution. The difference between the daily loan interest and the overdraft fee is substantial.

Important caution: Do this only as a safety net! DO NOT consider this an option if you are unable to control finances. You will only go deeper into debt.

526. *Another option to protect yourself from overdraft fees:* Instruct your bank to automatically transfer funds from your savings if you overdraw your account and to immediately notify you.

527. *Use only automatic teller machines that are networked into your bank's system.* It saves additional transaction fees.

528. *Think ahead before you use the automatic teller machine.* Do not run to the ATM several times in one day. Avoid multiple transaction fees.

529. *Anticipate special needs for cash.* Make special arrangements regarding ATM use if you need to increase your daily withdrawal limit due to a trip, etc.

530. *No transaction fees at ATMs?* Some banks offer a package that allows free transactions from ATMs. Ask.

531. *Should you use traveler's checks?* Many companies offer free traveler's checks. Guess why? Because they invest the balance of your unused traveler's checks—they don't need to pay out until the checks are cashed.

Going on that vacation of a lifetime? Let your money make interest for *you* while you are playing! Instead of carrying your funds in traveler's checks, leave your money in savings; use your credit card and ATMs.

Pay your credit card in full when you get home. You don't want to pay *them* interest!

532. *"Read your disclosures!!"* bellowed Muffie. (We had an animated interview.) "People do not read their mail! Any time your account is going to be negatively impacted in any way the bank must send you a 30-day notice."

Do you treat the stuffers in your bank statement like junk mail? Don't do that! Read your mail. All of it.

CREDIT

Just today Joe had a phone call. A persistent person offered him a pre-approved credit card. "By having another card you can increase your buying power, Mr. Yates!" "Increase your debt load" is more like it!

According to a booklet called *Out of Hock*, published by Dahlstrom & Company, Inc., Holliston, Massachusetts, nearly 110 million Americans have 950 million credit cards—nearly nine cards per person! During Christmas, Americans use the VISA card alone over 200 million times—about 5,500 times each minute!

Is credit okay? Should you even have a credit card? Should you *use* your credit card? Yes. Sensibly. A credit card is a way of establishing a good credit record. It saves you from carrying cash or checks on vacations or at other times. It enables you to order over the phone. And credit cards make it possible for you to purchase necessary items during a time of need. However, competition between credit companies is so fierce that cards are being offered to just about anyone, including the unemployed and college students. There is a *lot* of money made in interest!

Consolidation loans. What if it's already too late? How can you dig out of the debt pit? I am not a credit counselor or a financial wizard, but I know one thing: If you analyze your credit card debt and find that you are paying up to 18 percent (or more) on unpaid balances, it would be prudent to try to pay them off *as soon as possible*, even if it means borrowing money from another source at a much lower rate. This is one instance when taking a cash advance from another credit company might be sensible.

Example: I know a family that had accrued credit card debt of $4,000. This was on four different cards. Average interest payment was 15 percent. These people maintained excellent credit and tried to chip away at their debt by paying more than minimum—but they could never catch up. An offer for a no-fee card with low interest came in the mail. After careful examination of fine print and a few phone calls these folks used this card to pay off higher-interest cards (which were destroyed with great vigor) and went after their balance with gusto, saving bundles in interest. Then they locked the card away for emergency use and vowed to pay any balance in full each month.

National Foundation for Consumer Credit. "Read your mail!" bellowed Carol. Haven't we heard something like this already? Carol is a branch director for Consumer Credit Counseling Services, which is under the umbrella of the National Foundation for Consumer Credit. NFCC has "dedicated its efforts towards a better public understanding and use of consumer credit through programs of education, research and counseling."

As a consumer advocate and veteran of helping people out of debt, Carol has seen it all. I met with Carol and her associate, Greg. They told me about the pain and discouragement of people overcome with stress because of debt.

Carol and Greg insist that recognizing your financial difficulties is your biggest step. And it is usually taken at the mailbox. If you avoid reading your mail, it is the surest sign you are in trouble.

Are you avoiding your mail? Are you gripped with anxiety when the phone rings? Is pressure building from creditors? Has legal action been taken against you?

If you are overwhelmed with debt or if you just need someone to guide you through the maze of budgets, money management, and planned debt liquidation, these people might be able to help.

Consumer Credit Counseling Services is a not-for-profit organization with over seven hundred offices nationwide. Look in your Yellow Pages or call toll free for a location near you: 800-388-CCCS. Don't be scared. Be glad you are taking this biggest of all steps—by comparison, all others from now on will be tiny. You have faced your circumstances, so start your climb out of the pit by gladly putting one foot in front of the other. You can do it!

Credit record. "Check your credit report!" bellowed Greg. Credit bureaus receive reports on millions of people from several sources: credit card companies, banks, and stores, to name a few. Your credit record has detailed information: a list of addresses, jobs, information on your home, whether or not you rent, lists of credit accounts, closed accounts, terms and amounts of the accounts, payment history, loan data, and detail on revoked cards, lawsuits, bankruptcies, and so on.

Your credit record is critically important and should be reviewed periodically. Horror stories abound about mistaken identities or misinformation that ruined people's credit. Be sure yours is up-to-date and accurate.

There are three major credit bureaus: TRW, TransUnion, and Equifax. Call and ask which bureau your bank uses. Look in the Yellow Pages for the branch nearest you, call, and ask for a copy of your report. Expect to pay a small fee.

Make no mistake: ***A credit card is not money!*** A credit card is an IOU. It is your future money gone bye-bye. Used up. Kaput. Sayonara. See ya.

To help you become a sensible credit-card holder, consider these reminders:

533. Check your interest rate. Call Bankcard Holders of America (800-845-5000) for a free list of banks offering low interest cards.

534. Check your annual fee. Ask Bankcard Holders to tell you who offers no-fee cards.

535. Be leery of store credit cards. Almost all store credit cards have extremely high interest rates. No wonder they give a free bottle of pop when you sign up.

536. *Pay credit card balances in full!* If you pay them promptly, you will pay no interest. The minimum payment requested is best for them so they will make money on you.

537. *Take charge! Educate yourself.* You are the one responsible for the debt!

538. *Provide a good example for your children.* Teach your children about money management before it is too late.

539. *Do not live on credit.* Repeat after me: "Do not live on credit!"

540. *Do not use credit cards impulsively.* Want a method to avoid impulse? Take this tip from Carol: Put your credit card(s) in an empty mayonnaise jar. Fill three-quarters full with water. Freeze. This gives you a "cooling off" period before you use the card. Can't be microwaved, either, because the magnetic strip on the back would be damaged!

541. *A sure sign you are in trouble:* if you're charging groceries or incidentals such as movies.

542. *Know your legal responsibility if your credit card is lost or stolen.*

543. *Do not borrow money on your credit card* until you fully understand the interest method on cash advances.

544. ***Remember! Credit card debts are easier made than paid!***

INSURANCE

I was in the insurance business for a long time, and depended on client loyalty. Much can be said for a good insurance agent: someone who cares when you have a claim, someone who is concerned for your best interest, someone who reviews your policy regularly and finds ways to cut costs without cutting coverage. Loyalty is an important virtue; but with upward trends in insurance premiums, it is smart to consider other virtues, such as prudence, thriftiness, and sensible stewardship.

Home insurance. All insurance should be reviewed annually. On your homeowners insurance, look for the following:

545. *Make sure your home is not over- or underinsured* with the help of a trained agent.

546. *Consider everything*—special features (do you have oak cabinets or flooring?), decks, outbuildings, wood-stove, fireplace.

547. *Try to be insured for replacement value* on the house and personal belongings.

548. *Make certain you carry enough liability insurance to protect you from lawsuit.* Do you have a swimming pool? A crotchety old Cocker? Youngsters are attracted to dogs and pools. The law states that children must always be protected against themselves.

549. *Insure certain items separately.* Do you have fine art, guns, cameras, special collections, or musical equipment?

550. *Do you have extended theft coverage* to cover personal property stolen from your car or boat?

551. *Are you covered for business exposure in your home?* Day care that you offer? Incidental office? Farm liability?

552. *Some of you need to consider catastrophic coverage:* flood or earthquake insurance, or other.

553. *Are you getting credit for protective devices?* —smoke alarms, burglar alarms, fire extinguishers, dead-bolt locks?

554. *Does your company give other credit* for loss-free history, all-electric heat, no garage or outbuilding, or insuring your auto with them? Ask.

555. *Ask the price for different deductibles.* With our homeowner's policy, the premium difference between $250 and $500 deductible was meaningless. When we bumped it to $1,000, however, we saved a chunk of premium. Since we are careful not to submit small claims, a high deductible made sense. Our concern is catastrophe.

556. *Don't make lots of claims.* Insurance companies pay close attention to claims frequency, regardless how small the claim.

557. *Go over every inch of your policy and ask questions.* If your agent represents several companies, ask for comparisons. If not, you should shop for comparisons yourself. You may be in for a surprise.

Auto insurance. We recently left a company after eight claim-free and ticket-free years. The same coverage with another company saved over $500 a year! Review your auto coverage:

558. *Be certain you are charged correctly on each vehicle.* What kind of mileage and use is each rated for?

559. *Are you getting credit where you deserve it?* Are you credited for four-door, compact car, no claims, air-bags, multi-car, car alarm, homeowner's policy with same company?

560. *Do your young adults qualify for discounts*—driver-training or good-student discounts?

561. *Do you carry a sensible limit of liability?* What if you caused an accident with a van filled with people on their way to church? I insisted my clients carry $300,000 single limit of liability to cover bodily injury and property damage.

562. *Are your passengers protected against underinsured or uninsured motorists?*

563. *Do you have towing coverage?*

564. *Pay attention to deductibles.* Auto insurance deductibles might be controlled by your loan agreement, which states you must carry physical damage coverage (comprehensive and collision). Some lenders will not allow you to carry a higher-than-$500 deductible on collision. Comprehensive is commonly written with a $100 deductible. (Comprehensive covers fire, theft, windshields, and—in this part of the country—the all-important deer collision.)

565. *Review coverage on your older cars:* I frequently reviewed policies and found physical damage coverage on old vehicles. This is not always wise. Insurance companies try hard to stick to "book value" when settling claims. Are you insuring a "valueless vehicle"? Discuss this with your agent.

566. *Do you really want "automatic check withdrawal?"* Insurance companies offer a method of payment called "automatic check withdrawal." This method is appealing because the monthly premium is automatically withdrawn from your bank account: no monthly bill, no worry about lapse. This can be good, especially if you have a fixed premium rate.

Ribbet, ribbet, croak! Caution! Your intent is to control your finances, right? Once automatic check withdrawal is authorized, mistakes are rarely found, since you are not reviewing a monthly bill. Once authorized, your bank will pay whatever is requested each month. Premium payments might increase! Ever hear about the frog in water? He floats around happily as the water is slowly heated. The warm water soothes him—and, before he knows it, he is soup!

If you are on any kind of automatic withdrawal, check your bank statement carefully and monitor your expense!

Health insurance. Health insurance is a big concern for families today. And it is a big expense. National statistics tell us that 85 percent of Americans do carry some form of health insurance. Until there is a change in the existing system, I would make the following recommendations:

567. *Consult a reputable agent.*

568. *Consider high deductibles to cover catastrophe.* This means lower premiums.

569. *Understand policy limitations and co-insurance clauses.*

570. *Understand any pre-existing condition clause or exclusions on your policy.*

571. *Be aware of any waiting period on your policy.*

572. *Avoid most "specialty" policies* such as cancer policies, which are unnecessary because they duplicate coverage.

573. *Be certain you understand coverage for childbirth,* midwife or obstetrical services, and childbirth complications if you are of childbearing age.

574. *Check every single inch of medical bills,* most especially hospital bills. Do not be charged for services not received.

575. *If you have a claim that is denied, contest it.* Trust me.

576. *If you cannot meet the policy deductible or co-insurance requirements, tell your doctor.* Ask if it is possible to have your bill be limited to insurance payments.

577. *Find out if you have options on choice of company or coverage* if you have coverage through work. When comparing policy provisions, check coverage for such "extras" as mental health, addiction, or pregnancy. Compare prices.

Life insurance. There are basically two kinds of life insurance: whole-life (permanent) or term (temporary). Circumstances and age make a big difference on what kind you should buy. If you are determined to use your life insurance for protection *and* savings, then some version of a whole-life policy should be considered. If you are only interested in protection for a certain time, a term policy is your best bet.

Since my income is important to our budget, I carry ten-year renewable term. I like a ten-year term policy because the rate remains constant in ten-year increments. As the need for my income dwindles I have the option of reducing my insurance.

I stress my coverage because we overlook the contribution women make to the financial stability of families, whether they work at home or away from home. Mothers of young children, in particular, should consider some term coverage: It costs a bundle to care for children when something happens to Mom! Some financial consultants do not believe in buying insurance for children or young adults. I disagree. The loss of a young child is a tragedy and disruption to a family. Upon the death of a child, both parents will need time to adjust to this shock and will probably miss work. It is not the time for them to consider their budget. I urge everyone to consider a small term-rider for a child on Mom's or Dad's policy, if only for $5,000 or $10,000, so final expenses can be met.

Another reason I disagree pertains to young adults. We carried term insurance on Josh until he reached twenty-one. At that point we purchased a whole-life policy with a small monthly premium. Our reason was threefold: (1) We are protecting Joshua's insurability. The day will come when he needs insurance coverage due to family responsibility. Though unlikely, if something happened to him (heart attack, cancer, accident) to make him uninsurable, he is already covered. (2) The cost for whole-life at Josh's age is trifling compared to rates for an older man. (3) We are merely giving him a "jump start." One day we will turn the ownership over to him.

Budgets, banking, payments, insurance: It is one thing to talk about cheap bean recipes and quite another thing to face the harsh reality of monthly rent or mortgage, isn't it?

This has been a somewhat somber chapter—perhaps the chapter we wish we didn't have to read, yet the one we need to read most. Don't be discouraged.

If you are determined to get out of debt or live a thrifty lifestyle you *must* persevere. Pick yourself up. Dust yourself off. Steady as you go. Each inch of your progress will eventually become a tentative step, each step a stride. Keep your course. You can do it!

TEN

Resourceful Recreation

This is the fun part! We get to talk about things to do just to have fun. Even Grim likes this section!

I wonder if we have much real fun anymore, or are we driven, determined to participate in an activity or sport because it is popular, determined to buy expensive toys or equipment because ads promise adventure. Are some of us paying dearly to keep up with the hype? Are we so far removed from genuine recreation that we chase in circles and bounce from one frenzied activity to another in pursuit of pleasure?

Or do our children zone out in front of the TV, hour after hour, bleary-eyed, letting good sunshine or a yard piled with leaves go to waste? Stop and listen to what I am trying to say: My underlying message is for you to fully grasp biblical principles as you manage your affairs ***and*** turn to simpler, gentler times. There are many forms of recreation which don't involve investing a fortune in equipment or toys.

Ever looked for something right under your nose? Ever heard the statement "Not seeing the forest for the trees?" Discover your hometown! Think locally.

$uper $avers

578. *Check Friday's newspaper for weekend happenings.* Do not be picky! If a group puts together a free demonstration of old engines and cars, take the kids. If a park is having a pet show, put a tutu on the spaniel and bring the camera. If the mall is having a trade show, wander around and collect free samples. If a museum is having a lecture, make a date with your mate. If a band is playing music, go do the polka. If a county fair is coming, challenge your children to enter cookies.

579. *Check church calendars.* Churches are sources of endless free and wholesome recreation. Do not be tied down to your denomination! Watch the church section in the newspaper or talk to friends from other churches. Films, activity nights, and concerts are always offered in my area.

580. *Check into lectures* if a college or university is nearby. Joe and I drive to a lecture at the University of Montana one night each month. Experts from around the globe speak on a variety of issues.

581. *Volunteer as an usher for local theater productions.* Get to see the show for free. (Get to *memorize* the show for free.)

582. *Call local firms and ask if they will give your family a tour or demonstration.* Who could you call? Some of you live near factories and manufacturing plants. Others live in less-developed areas but could call the bakery, grocery store, TV or radio station, police or fire department.

583. *Renew your library card.* Has your library card expired? Renew! Rediscover the resources at your library. Teach children to respect this place and bring them regularly.

584. *Designate a library night for the whole family.* Dad may curl up in a corner for a snooze with a pile of newspapers and that's okay.

585. *Rediscover reading as recreation.* What is your pleasure? Magazines, cookbooks, newspapers, novels, encyclopedias, nonfiction. It is all in the library. And more.

586. *Bring your little children to reading hour.* Nearly every library has a time when youngsters are entertained. If yours doesn't—volunteer.

587. *Research a topic (maybe a country) as a family.* Teach your kids to access reference material; let the librarian help you. (I sure need help in these days of computers!)

588. *Borrow a record or a tape.* Did you read right? Yep. Libraries are a good source for music. Borrow the "1812 Overture" and let it thunder through your home. Borrow Brahms to soothe everyone afterwards. Use this to teach your children about some of the masters of music.

589. *Borrow a video.* Our main library has a vast assortment of videos, from National Geographic specials to every conceivable "how-to." Cooking videos, travel videos, home improvement videos: They are all there.

590. *Take home an armload of magazines.* Many libraries have a shelf or two marked "free."

591. *Check the bulletin board for lectures or clubs of interest.* Ask if the library is going to show a film or slide show.

592. *No time to read? Borrow a "book-on-tape."*

593. *Enjoy the peace and quiet of the library.* Leave the world on the street. Slip into your library to sit quietly with your thoughts. Teach children the value of silence.

594. *Go for a walk.* Do you know what we do? We stop the car in a random neighborhood and walk around the block. Hand in hand. Does that sound strange to you? There are some cultures in our world that find a stroll during the day or after dinner vital. Are you like Grim, who goes Zoom!Zoom!? Slow down. Experience the magic and soul-soothing pleasure of walking.

There are times I think people these days are positively insane. We have even turned our *walking* into intense exercise: swinging dumbbells, wearing appropriate walking costumes, breathing correctly, and sporting the latest pricey walking shoes. Puh-leeze. Grab the dog, tear the kids away from that awful television, handcuff your husband to your waistband, and get going. Explore your neighborhood. Or one across town. Walk through a cavernous business area after everyone has gone home. Sit by a creek. Watch boats come through locks. Kick sand. Skip rocks. Pick up litter as you go. Maybe even walk to the library.

595. *Share your discoveries.* A creative child could approach a local newspaper and ask about doing a monthly travel column: articles about areas and neighborhoods, attractions and businesses in your town.

596. *Take a hike!* There is great pleasure and reward in family hiking. Steve and Kristin take hikes with their kids. They bring along a special treat for energy (see box).

Trail Mix

Ingredients in descending order of quantity:

Generic toasted oat cereal
Dried fruit cut into small pieces, or raisins
Sunflower seeds (buy raw, unsalted seeds in bulk)
Chocolate chips
Mini pretzels
Odds 'n' ends.

Tip: Let children assemble the trail mix. Friend Jo says measuring ingredients strengthens their math skills.

597. *Have a picnic!* Everyone likes a picnic! This is an inexpensive way to have fun because you can use food on hand and picnic right at home. A picnic can be spontaneous and held any time

of year. What do you need? An old blanket or sheet, a jug of lemonade or a thermos of hot chocolate, and whatever the kids assemble in the kitchen. Leave it up to them. You can even spread a blanket on the floor or set up a tent in your living room and picnic in the middle of winter!

598. *Winter play.* Why not develop your own version of this favorite activity of ours:

We have a squadron of volunteer "elves" who decorate our three-block downtown with thousands of Christmas lights for a sparkling display. Joe and I invite friends to meet us after dark, at one end of the street. We tell our guests to dress warmly, greet them with a thermos of hot cocoa, and take them on a stroll through shops lining the street. Church carolers volunteer their voices, a one-horse sleigh trots back and forth, merchants offer snacks, and rosy-cheeked friends come along home for hot chili and homemade cornbread. Sure beats the movies.

599. *Simple fun.* Jo and Larry have three children. Add four extra one weekend. All seven kids (under ten) were packed into their faithful family car and hauled to our school athletic field. Two five-year-olds ran laps, two older children took up with horses in an adjoining pasture, the others bounced on pads left over from pole-vault practice. Throw in a few bats and gloves and you have the makings of an utterly delightful afternoon. Miles from home: four. Money spent: $0. Not a bad outing.

600. *Plant a garden.* Give each child a pack of seeds and responsibility for a particular crop. Have a family fair at the end of the season; invite relatives and friends. Award ribbons.

601. *Go fly a kite.* After you make it.

602. *"Dig to China" in the backyard with your children.* Fancy lawn? Grass grows fast. So do kids.

603. *Build your own mini-golf course in the yard.*

604. *Old detergent bottles make great squirt guns* and take the "gun" out of the squirt.

605. *Cook together.* Do something crazy in the kitchen; have pizza for breakfast and ice cream pie for dinner.

606. *Write a family cookbook* with a particular theme: "Hamburgers, Hash, and Holidays by the Ferpel Family of Fine Cooks." Give the book as a Christmas gift.

607. *Search thrift stores or garage sales for a "special plate."* Do this as a family. Be sure you find a unique plate. Use the plate for your guest of honor... Jesus! Give children full rein in setting a special place for Him. The plate can double for honored guests on birthdays, Mother's Day, etc.

608. *Dress for dinner.* Hunt local rummage sales or thrift stores with your children for dress-up clothes. Everyone get dressed in something funny for dinner some night.

609. *Put life in the Gospels!* Don't just talk to your children about "Living Water." Take them to a lake or stream.

610. *Build a sand (or mud) castle and blast it* with the garden hose. Teach boys and girls the importance of foundations (Matthew 7:24-27).

611. *Send children on a hunt to find something from nature that glorifies the Lord.* Ask them to explain why they made their choice. Use this time to explain that the creation is separate from the Creator (Romans 1:25). One child once returned with a neighbor's basset hound!

612. *Get rid of TV or cable altogether.* We went for three years without TV during our son's adolescent years. When I look back I see an active, happy family.

613. *Share the savings of eliminating cable TV.* Steve suggests dividing cable TV savings between each child. For example: If there are three children in the family and cable costs $15 a month, each child gets $5. This money can be put in savings, a special fund, or spent wisely. Children must learn sensible stewardship, too.

614. *Create TV traditions.* Leslie's family rents a family video to watch while eating "smorgasbord" on Friday night. Each fam-

ily member chooses one or two items. This is a good tip as long as Junior doesn't pick shrimp cocktail!

615. *Build a campfire pit in your backyard.* Sit, sing, and roast marshmallows.

616. *Encourage music or voice lessons* if your child is so inclined. (Good application for cable TV savings!) A music teacher in elementary school met with Josh a half-hour each week for years... at no cost! Check with your school to see if this is possible. Note: Do not expect or demand services for free! Our offer to pay for the lessons was declined.

617. *Go to a quality Christian concert as a family.* (Eat oatmeal for a week to save up the money.) Don't feel bad if older children do not sit with you. And bring something to protect your ears!

618. *Prom Night alternatives.* Is there a parent alive who doesn't worry about safety on Prom Night? Do something about it! We organized a Prom Day/Night/Early Morning and kept kids busy from start to finish.

Midday: The young couples met in a parking lot and were given a list of "duties" to perform. Among other things, they had to find ten items on a treasure hunt (you think it's *easy* to find red linoleum?), bowl two games and save the score, figure out the "mystery" flavor at a local ice cream store, and compete at a video game parlor.

Before prom: Once dressed, the kids met again, were "toasted" with sparkling cider and hauled to a home for a royal banquet—complete with harpist (who donated her talent)! Next came the prom, which was a dud compared to the fun they had had elsewhere. Next came dessert at another home, where prizes were awarded to the treasure hunt winners. Next came carloads of kids to our lake home for breakfast at 3 A.M. Guess what? They fell asleep! Joe and I ate sausage and eggs for weeks.

Sixteen of our precious children had an alcohol-free, sex-free Prom Night... we call that money well spent.

Holidays. Holidays can be costly, can't they? Family expectations can be high. And yet there are inexpensive ways to celebrate meaningfully.

619. *Keep holidays simple.* Bring peace into holy days. Plan to keep things peaceful. Work at keeping things simple.

620. *Keep the Fourth of July, Memorial Day, and Labor Day patriotic.* Terry and Pat take their youngsters to a cemetery on Memorial Day. The children bring lilacs to place on undecorated graves.

621. *Have a Passover meal on the Thursday before Easter.* Explain to your children this would be typical of the Last Supper. Jesus certainly would have eaten honey cakes. Try a new recipe for this occasion (see below).

Honey Cake

4 c. flour
2 tsp. baking powder
1/4 tsp. baking soda
1 tsp. cinnamon
1/2 tsp. ground cloves
3 eggs
1/2 c. sugar
1 c. honey
4 Tbs. oil
1 c. strong cold coffee
1/2 c. chopped nuts

Combine the flour, baking powder, baking soda, and spices. In a separate bowl beat eggs. Add sugar and honey and beat. Add oil. Alternate adding dry ingredients and coffee; mix well. Add nuts. Pour into two well-greased 9" x 5" bread pans. Bake 45 minutes at 350°F.

622. *Make hot cross buns during Holy Week.*

623. *Make a Yule Log with Advent candles.* Level off the bottom of a foot-long, thick branch. Drill four holes for Advent candles. Decorate with non-flammable ornaments.

624. *Make a crèche out of children's clay.*

625. *Teach giving instead of receiving.* As a child I shared a portion of my holiday candy with children at a nearby orphanage. It became an important event for me to bag up my candy and present it to the lady at the door.

626. *I heartily recommend that children be taken to shut-ins* and nursing homes and that the children pass out treats they have made.

627. *Celebrate fall instead of Halloween.* Instead of carving a pumpkin, make pumpkin people. Draw faces on pumpkins and stuff old clothes like scarecrows.

628. *Find a local church that has a creative alternative for Halloween,* perhaps an indoor carnival.

629. *A group of friends or relatives can throw a wacky party for their children.* There is an abundance of suggestions in youth workers' handbooks, which can be borrowed from church.

630. *Find a barn and turn Halloween into a hoedown.* Or turn your garage into a barn. Get a bale of straw, borrow someone's pony, a chicken or two; serve cupcakes and cider.

631. *Pick out a "Family Festival Day" to celebrate each year.* Give thanks to the Lord for your unique and special family.

ELEVEN

Eating Out

Want to save money? Stay home and cook. Zip by the arches, forgo the tacos, and turn your car toward home. Not so easy, you say. After all, you have to drive Suzy and Fred to dance lessons, drop off Matt for baseball, do all those errands. It is just plain silly to expect you to cook, right?

So make a sandwich. Where is it written that dinner has to be a hot meal? Where is it written that children's growth will be stunted if they munch on vegies in the back seat?

632. *First rule for saving money when eating out: Don't.* The nutritional value is questionable, the fat and salt levels are out of sight, the cost skyrocketing.

Am I saying you should never go to a restaurant? Certainly not! I am suggesting you return to a previous era when a restaurant visit was a treat or special occasion. Get out of the habit of using the drive-through for the sake of convenience. And remember! Mute the commercials! Advertisers know what they are doing when they promote giveaways for your children. If the kids want to slide and swing, take them to a park. If they want every new toy or gadget that comes along, you had better have a long talk with yourself and think about your never-satisfied little consumer.

But, how *do* you save money when you *do* eat out?

$uper $avers

633. *Save restaurant visits for special occasions.*

634. *"Keep the change."* I remember perching on a stool at Woolworth's when I was little, next to my mother. She told me I could have anything I wanted providing I did not spend more than $1. I knew Woolworth's menu by heart! Inflation has left its mark, but this is still a good idea. If you want to give the family a treat, take them someplace and limit each one to a certain amount, say $3. Let the children take ownership and learn a bit about financial management to boot: Let them keep the change.

635. *Sweets to the sweet.* Want to get dressed up and go out for a special date with your mate? Pick a fine restaurant, call for a reservation, explain that your funds are limited and that this is a special treat—then go for a fancy dessert and a cup of coffee! I have done this, and establishments have obliged by providing romantic tables and good service.

636. *Speaking of good service—thrifty does not mean stingy.* Tip your server!

637. *Ask the restaurant if you and your husband or child can split a plate.* This works well in places that sell spaghetti. There may be a fee for the extra plate, but this gives you a chance to dine out without breaking the bank.

638. *Do not buy appetizers.* Let me say that again: *Do not buy appetizers.* The bread or rolls served in advance of your meal will tide you over.

639. *Use coupons.* Some merchant groups offer coupon books for a fee which give many two-for-one deals at restaurants. Check with your chamber of commerce.

640. *Radio stations periodically have auctions.* One nearby station offers food certificates for local restaurants at reduced rates.

641. *Avoid dinner altogether.* Go to a nice place for breakfast or lunch. Some places let you purchase from the lunch menu in

the evening. Ask questions—politely, of course. Joseph and I go for coffee (and sometimes a sweet roll) on Saturday morning. We try to treat ourselves every week and look forward to Saturday coffee with glee.

Since Joe and I met during a breakfast-time, each May 7 we have breakfast for dinner to celebrate the anniversary of our meeting. We normally go to a restaurant that will oblige our curious request. This year we decided to have a campfire, make cowboy coffee and rolls, and fry some bacon. That way we creatively circumvented a trip to town and a $10-$15 expense. All my husband had to do was... bring home the bacon!

642. *Drink water.* Milk, pop, beer, and wine are expensive in restaurants. Ask for a wedge of lemon and some ice and sip away.

643. *OK, let's talk about pizza.* You know, that gift from God we cannot get enough of... pizza! Pizza costs plenty, doesn't it? Make your own!

Pizza Dough

1-1/2 tsp. yeast, warm water
1/2 tsp. salt
3-1/2 c. flour (as needed to make "elastic" dough)

Combine yeast and water and let sit until you see foam. Combine salt and flour, add yeast-water, and knead until you have a glistening ball of dough. Put dough in a bowl that has been oiled well (a deep bowl with sides so the dough has "something to climb!"); cover. Let it rise for a couple of hours. Punch down dough and knead a few minutes. This makes one thick crust or two thin ones. It can also be spread in a jelly-roll pan.

Pizza Topping

This is limited only to your imagination and taste, but here is a budget version:

Shmear a coating of oil on surface of dough, then spread with a can of tomato sauce which has been liberally seasoned with basil and oregano. Thoroughly drain a can of sliced mushrooms and distribute. Bake at 375°F for 20 minutes; then dust with grated mozzarella or any cheese you have on hand. Return it to the oven for 5 or 10 minutes to melt the cheese.

644. ***Lunch, coffee and $weet rolls.*** Do you "do lunch"? And you are trying to save money?! Pack your own! Bring a brown bag! Do anything, but ***don't do lunch!***

Story time.

I leave for work each morning while the world sleeps; Joe leaves an hour later than I. One cold day he appeared at the door where I was working. He held a cup of take-out coffee. "Roses," said Joe, as he handed me that steaming treat. At that moment, it was even *better* than flowers. What a delight! Off he drove (with his own cup) as I settled on a chair and sipped the coffee in the quiet of early morning. Soon I was anticipating "roses" every day. Until I added it up: five days a week at $1 a day = $5. $5 times 52 weeks = $260 a year! On something I didn't need, nice as it was!

Spending $5 on lunch every day? That is $1300 each year! Spending $7 between lunch and coffee break? A cool $1820! Are you reading this book because you want to be more careful with your money? ***Don't do lunch!***

645. ***Sometimes you gotta do lunch!*** Just the other day, Grim and I were stuck in town. And hungry. I drove to the supermarket.

Grim sulked as I whizzed past the ready-made sandwiches and the deli. I had to drag him from the cookie section.

Out to the car I marched with six succulent strawberries and a fresh-from-the-oven miniature loaf of seven-seed bread. Total: 88¢.

"You see, Grim," I said, as I ripped off a chunk of bread, "we need the chromium found in whole grains."

"So go lick a bumper," said my petulant friend.

I stuck a strawberry in his mouth.

TWELVE

Grab-bag Getaways

Are there some things you neglect, particularly because of lack of funds? Do the words "vacation," "play," or "leisure" come to mind? Do responsibilities stand as roadblocks to rest and recreation, trapping you in a weary cycle of work and obligation?

If you overlook or postpone rest, read Hebrews 4:9-11: "There remains, then, a Sabbath-rest for the people of God; for anyone who enters God's rest also rests from his own work, just as God did from his. Let us, therefore, make every effort to enter that rest." Not only does God tell us to rest, He *created* rest.

When did you last truly rest?

"Hah!" Is that what you are thinking? If it is, rest awhile now. Turn this chapter into adventure; look into its ideas with curiosity and enthusiasm.

Joe and I ran into the "responsibility roadblock" all too often. It was easy to get past the blockade—we just brainstormed our way through! Maps, addresses of friends, books about our area, letters to chambers of commerce—all helped us creatively find a way around our money crunch and take time to play. A map, a vacation budget, and a letter put us in Canada one November for a tuba concerto! We rarely "vacate" long, often taking extended weekend opportunities. I share this one exception with you to demonstrate the power of creative planning:

One week in October. Our holiday started with three nights in a remote cabin two hours north of town. Prudently, we did not rely on our fishing skill and brought food from home. Cost for lodging? Free from friends. Cost for food? Minimal. Cost for recreation? Two fishing licenses. Day four sent us two hours south of home to our son's apartment in a university town. After a free lecture the three of us went to a coffee house. Cost for lodging? Free stay with Josh. Cost for food? Minimal. Cost for recreation? Three espressos: $4.50. Next day we zigged and zagged our way through backroads to a famous mining community in our state, where we visited friends. Cost for lodging? Free stay with friends. Cost for food? Nothing. Cost for recreation? Nothing. Next day we explored our way to a friend's home in another part of the state and stayed the night. Cost same as above. The final night was in our state capital. We toured government buildings and slept at an inexpensive motel.

Throughout those days Joe and I rediscovered each other, exclaimed repeatedly over the beauty of our state, laughed and talked with friends, stopped to sit by streams.

Your vacation weeks. This chapter discusses different types of travel and holidays with an eye toward frugality. Not every suggestion is cost-free. Yet, even if you can afford the luxury, finding a bargain rate on a trip is sensible. Some need incentive (and convincing) that an overnight trip to a friend's spare bedroom is sensible, too.

Let's suppose you have been frugal all year and amassed a fortune. You are determined to take that long overdue honeymoon or to take your children to a zoo two thousand miles away. There are times when you have to depend on others to know your prices!

TRAVEL AGENTS

It is not wasteful to take your family on a trip or vacation. It can be sensible, educational, and remedial. It is wasteful if you do not put effort into finding the "path of least expenditure." If you are planning a trip to a faraway location, you may need the help of a travel agent. I did... for this book. I called Dottie. This is what she said:

Travel agents have buying power. They also have access to airline computers, usually know of bargains, and can acquire information about specialty tours. Most agents have *lots* of data; some have reference or video libraries. Go to a reputable agent. Explain your circumstance. Ask if he or she will "package" your trip for you. Ask about fees before you request service. Normally, a travel agent's commission comes from ticket sales.

Touring. Many travel professionals insist that touring is the best way to go. Most significantly, you know in advance what your cost will be—and you can usually find a tour that matches your interests and pocketbook. For safety reasons, touring is particularly good for women alone or with children. Tours often offer children's rates and are usually insured. Touring is cheaper than most independent travel for two reasons: (1) Tour operators buy in volume and (2) tour operators have working relationships with hotels, services, transporters, etc.

Package travel. There is a recent development within the tour industry. Tour companies will now arrange your independent itinerary, including hotel and car rental, usually at lower rates than you can obtain. There is a fee, which is generally offset by savings. A call to the National Tour Association (800-755-TOUR) is free and will point you to tour directors in your area.

MODES OF TRAVEL

Recreational vehicles. Renting a motor home may sound expensive at first, but if you want to take your clan on a trip, this is a money-saving consideration. Rental agents are found in nearly all states and offer a variety of vehicle sizes. When using an RV you must factor in the cost of gas and plan ahead for trailer parks if you need hookups, especially during summer months. Traveling in an RV certainly takes a lot of stress out of a holiday, liberating you from the airport/ train/motel shuffle. Put your clothes and food in your traveling home and off you go! A brochure produced by the Recreation Vehicle Rental Association claims that motorhome travel is economical. Units available from rental agencies can include motorhomes, mini motorhomes, van conversions, travel trailers, truck campers, and folding camping trailers. A booklet produced by the association is thorough in explaining RV rental. The booklet also discusses aspects of motorhome travel including operation, information about driver's licenses, even campground courtesy. A local travel agent might loan this booklet. To order it, call 800-336-0355. There is a fee.

Frequent flier programs. A frequent flier program is sort of like "buy one, get one free": For every mile you fly, you get credit for other miles some other time. Obviously, if you fly often you can benefit immensely. Did you know you need not fly often—or ***at all***—to earn credit for free airline travel? It's true. At this writing all frequent flier programs with major U.S. airlines offer free membership with no minimum number of flights. Frequent flier programs give credit for car rentals, motel stays, and credit card usage. Some allow mileage credit for long-distance phone calls! Call the 800 operator, get the number of your airline of choice, and give them a jingle. You might qualify for a trip through the "friendly skies."

Trains. Unless you are paying for special accommodations, such as a sleeper car, train travel is usually less costly than airfare. Amtrak rates go up a bit in summer, but tickets have no restrictions: You may change your return date without penalty, you do not have to stay through a Saturday night for good rates, and there are no advance purchase requirements. It is good to book well in advance before a busy time, however, since Amtrak has a certain "block" of tickets selling for lower fare. Waiting 'til November to book Christmas travel might land you a higher rate. Children age two to fifteen travel for half-fare; under two for free. People sixty-five or older are entitled to a 15 percent discount. Train travel is fun. Children are able to move around and trains often have sight-seeing cars. Pack your own food or you are at the mercy of train fare. All aboard!

Bus. Of course, if you are really looking for frugal transportation, you could leave the driving to them. Bus travel is still an excellent buy *if* you are not constrained by time, you can sit for long periods without discomfort, you can sleep in a recliner, and you do not care who sits next to you. It can be an adventure in itself!

Car travel. Before you travel by car: 1. Study a map. Check all available routes. Know where you can buy gas or make potty stops. 2. Learn about your route. Unless you like to go "zoom!" like Grim, take detours. Leave the interstate every now and then—visit a museum, enjoy a vista, swing in a park. Joe and I rarely travel anyplace without diverting through a small town or a neighborhood, just to explore. 3. Make sure you thoroughly check your car: tire condition and proper inflation, all fluids OK, check all belts. Keep water and oil in the trunk, along with flares and a blanket.

646. *Travel by car cuts expenses dramatically.* Beside savings, an advantage is freedom to stop and go as you please. Lines at air or train terminals are eliminated, as well as the shuttle to your motel. With a car you can usually go straight to your destination.

Unless you are tent or trailer camping, you need to develop "motel savvy" before you hit the road (see hints below). And boredom is a challenge as you zip along interstates and byways, especially for children. Here are a few games to take the bore out, for a little while at least. The Yates family has refined each of these games to an art form!

647. *Quest:* Our family invented the game. It can be played by two people, but teams of two or three make it especially fun (and loud, I'm afraid...). Make a list of ten items. Each team has the

same list. The first team to find all items on the list wins. Simple. Until you include things like: mule, yellow car, woman with red hair, black and white dog, car with two bicycles on top. (Or the more advanced: yellow car with Nebraska plates, two bicycles on top, pulling camping trailer, driven by woman with red hair.) Caution: Be sure the driver can handle sudden screams, excessive argument, and debate.

648. *Alphabet:* We play this anytime, even driving to town for groceries. The game is not always competitive; at times we play alone. The object is to find words that begin with the alphabet, consecutively. First one who gets to "Z" wins. We omit X. For instance, if I see a "rest area" sign I shout "area!" for "A" and so forth. Catch: Other players cannot use the same word. In other words, "area" cannot be used again.

649. *Another alphabet game:* Consecutively go through the alphabet, taking turns. First person: "I am going to Arizona on an Antelope to be an Accountant." Next person would say same sentence using "B" words and so forth.

650. *License plates:* Everyone keeps track of different states' plates; the person with the greatest number of states wins.

651. *Questions:* Sometimes we pass time by asking questions. Questions such as: What is your favorite cereal? What is your favorite flavor ice cream? What is your favorite color? What is your favorite song? This is a pleasant way to establish communication and even greater understanding.

Travel scams. When something sounds too good to be true, whether a trip to the Caribbean or a furniture sale, it probably is—too good to be true. In other words: gimmick. Sometimes gimmick translates another way: scam. The National Tour Association offers preventive advice:

- Use credit card or check when booking.
- If using cash, get a receipt.
- Ask about "errors, omissions, and liability" insurance. Shady char-

acters do not carry insurance!

- Ask for client references.
- Call the chamber of commerce or Better Business Bureau if uncertain.
- Never use 900 numbers. Request a local number; this establishes that the company has a central office.

652. *A swimming pool is answered prayer for people traveling with children.* Find the least expensive motel with a pool and be certain the pool is open and operating.

653. *What if there's no pool?* Does the town where you are staying (or one nearby) offer public swimming accommodations? Are they free? Let the kids de-energize and clean up while you stretch your legs. Or go to a YMCA.

654. *Opt for the less expensive motel* if you are near a body of water with a public beach.

655. *Plan ahead.* Do a bit of planning and research. Study a map and highlight your route. Most major hotel/motel chains have 800 phone numbers; call and check prices.

656. *Motels often cost more in metropolitan or resort areas.* Thirty miles down the road the same chain may be less expensive.

657. *Know your prices!* "Kids stay free" means nothing if you are paying a high price in comparison to other motels.

658. *Tell the clerk you have a limited budget; ask for help to keep costs down.* Can you add cots? Can you put small ones on the floor in sleeping bags? If you are not getting much help, speak to the manager.

659. *Don't order room service!*

660. *Do NOT make calls from your room phone!* Go to the public phone in the lobby. Why? Lots of motels superimpose a fee on phone rates. No kidding.

661. *Make motel reservations and secure them with your credit card,* even during the off season. Why? Read on: Scenario #1) Joe and I could not find a room on five hundred miles of Montana

"high line" because of tourists. We slept in our car. Frugal, but our bodies hated us for days. Scenario #2) Same situation. All we found was a room in a dingy motel. And was it ever! Scenario #3) We traveled to a distant town soon after Mama died. We had cared for her in our home for months and were physically and emotionally spent. Car trouble added to our misery. All we wanted was a bed. No problem in October, right? Wrong—state teachers' convention. We ended up with the bridal suite in an expensive motel.

662. *Sometimes a motel might be less costly than staying with friends.* If you feel obliged to reciprocate hospitality by taking friends out to dinner, for instance, a friendly "Hihowareyou" phone call while you are in town might be more prudent.

663. *Take the pits out of pit stops!* Gasoline stations do not sell gas anymore. Gasoline stations sell every conceivable convenience food concocted by man. Think about it: When is the last time you stopped for gas while traveling and did not walk away with a bag of chips or a pop? Talk about impulse buying! Dollar bills slip through your fingers on this one. Pack your own snacks. Pass around celery filled with cream cheese or dried apple slices while you travel. Save a homemade brownie for gas stops. Drag out your water jug or your own can of pop, bought for a third of the price back home.

664. *Food is food.* Joe and I seldom visit fast-food restaurants when we travel. We wander through supermarkets. We buy bulk cheese, a loaf of French bread, a banana to split. A jug of water takes care of thirst. We have picnicked in malls, parks, alongside the road, at rest stops, in parking lots, even driving over the Continental Divide in a snowstorm!

665. *Look for big trucks in the parking lot.* Sure sign of an inexpensive restaurant.

666. *Let dessert be a frozen treat on a stick* at the next pit stop (just this once!).

667. *Ask if plates of food can be shared.*

668. *Tank up on H_2O.* Your child will not develop rickets if water accompanies a meal instead of milk.

669. *A bowl of pasta is often less expensive* and significantly more filling and satisfying than most restaurant fare.

Creative vacations. Give your vacation a creative send-off as you and your family or friends brainstorm alternatives. Pile everyone on the bed to eat popcorn while someone "mans" the pad and pencil. Use hints from this chapter as ideas and challenge each other to develop strategies for some penny-pinching pilgrimages.

670. *Cruise ships offer bargains off-season.* Or cruise on a barge or freighter! You will save a bundle on evening clothes alone.

671. *Colleges, organizations, and churches regularly offer travel deals.*

672. *Host a foreign exchange student—bring the country to your home.* Best bet: Send *your* child on an exchange program. Josh went to Japan. He still handles chopsticks with aplomb.

673. *Do you have a friend or relative* who would let you plop a sleeping bag on the floor? Or use a sleeper couch? I bet you do! This might not be the thing to do for a romantic interlude, but it sure takes the sting out of travel. Incidentally, this offer works both ways!

674. *"Trade" homes* for a few weeks with someone from another state or country.

675. *Send the kids to Grandma's for the night.* Make popcorn and cuddle with your mate on your *own* sleeper couch!

676. *Try elder or youth hostels.* Check your library for locations. These places offer lodging at bargain rates and very often admit folks of all ages.

677. *Women might rent a motor home for a few days* and take their children to the woods or to a campground with structured activity. Bonus: You take your own food.

678. *Pitch in with another couple and rent a cabin.*

679. *Take your family to a working ranch in Wyoming!*

680. *Consider a bed and breakfast.* Some offer a less expensive package than motel plus restaurant. Libraries have directories of regional B and Bs.

681. *Enter travel contests.*

682. *Use the local transit system for cheap travel* (after you have checked with the chamber of commerce or police department for safety).

683. *Always carry a small electric hot pot* and a couple packages of dry soup, hot cocoa, oatmeal.

684. *Check with convention centers or chambers of commerce to discover what is free in town,* especially for children. There is usually lots to do.

685. *Become a missionary.* Is a local church or parachurch organization sending a mission delegation to another state or country? What a great vacation!

686. *Check with Habitat for Humanity* for a nearby project on which your entire family can help.

687. *Create your own mission project.* Ask your pastor if someone is in need. A widow? A single mom? Plan your "vacation" as a family; get everyone involved. Beautify a yard, paint a building, clean a house. Bet you get chocolate chip cookies in the deal!

688. *Organize a travel club.* This one's a $uper $aver: Get together with other families and friends. Pick one country each month; assemble together after all have researched the "destination." Serve ethnic food, wear ethnic clothing, practice different customs. Go to your library or travel agent to borrow a video about your "destination." Travel as far as your creativity will take you.

689. *Go camping!* Bring your home into the woods or alongside a lake—go camping cheaply. Make cowboy bedrolls using bungee cords or rope. An air mattress and a few blankets will do. Pack peanut butter sandwiches for breakfast.

    Go as unencumbered as possible. Bring a plastic tarp in case of rain. Consider a few things in advance: bugs, safety, fire restrictions, weather. Yes, it is nice if you have a lot of gear. But gear costs money; why are you camping in the first place? Camp to relax, to wade, to talk, not talk, to play rummy, to read, to explore, to fish, to sing, to think about vacation roadblocks—and giggle.

690. *Home on the range.* State and federal campsites dot our countryside. Call your state board of tourism or the U.S. Forest Service for information.

691. *Entertainment for adults and children abounds at many privately owned campsites:* bingo, square dancing, games, nature talks, nature walks. They usually have hot showers, laundry facilities, and camp stores.

692. *Write for a "camping vacation planner"* (which emphasizes RV camping) from: Go Camping America, P.O. Box 2669, Reston, VA 22090-0669.

693. *Can't afford a campground or one not available?* Call a local pastor and ask if he knows where you can "set up" for the night. Better yet, ask if you can use the backyard of his church. Or drive to the police station. Or ask a farmer. Note: Be extremely courteous and quiet. Leave the place clean. Use a service station for hygiene.

694. *Some stores sell tents large enough to sleep a family for the cost of one night's motel.* How else can you get a tent? Read on....

695. *Watch "penny-saver" ads and the classifieds for tent ads.*

696. *Purchase your own want ad.* Be specific as to size and type of tent desired.

697. *Listen to radio swap and sell programs.* A tent or other camping equipment might be offered.

698. *Be a shrewd tent-shopper.* Know your prices and be sure you get a tent that is bug-proof and waterproof, with a ground cover and zippers that work.

699. *If all else fails, buy two polywhatchamagig tarps* and some clothesline or bungee cords. Bring bug spray.

THIRTEEN

Car Savvy: Purchase with Purpose

"We don't buy what we can afford; we buy what we want," observed Hank. Hank sells cars. And his words are tough, but true. It doesn't seem to matter if it is a car, a winter jacket, or a roast beef sandwich. Do you buy what you can afford, or do you buy what you want? Hank sees it all the time: If the monthly outlay is within reason, it's a done deal. "Sell me that red beauty with the stick on the floor. And throw in a good stereo. And air. Don't forget air."

Of all the chapters I have written, none has affected me as this one has. It has disturbed me to confront the entire picture of car ownership: sticker price, accessory price, dealer price, interest, insurance, warranty, maintenance, more gasoline, break-down, more interest, more gasoline, tires, interest, monthly payments, upkeep....

I turned to Grim in dismay: "How can anybody save money with a car?!" I asked, almost in anguish.

"Can't," is his arresting, and honest, reply.

Can you save money owning a car, or is it a losing proposition? Well, that depends. It depends on how you perceive car ownership. Some people consider car payments a fact of life and upgrade routinely. Some people regard car payments as a trap and keep "old faithful" on its tires as long as possible. Others feel that since a car is necessary, they will do their best to cut costs in purchase, maintenance, and operation. This chapter is written with that position in mind.

Needless to say, the easiest way to save money on a car is not to own one. Or to strategically drive the one you have. Since very few of us can get along without a car, we should look at ways to cut back on our dependence. What are some viable alternatives to driving?

Walk. If you live within a mile of your school or workplace, and if it is safe, walk. Same goes for groceries. An average person can walk one mile in fifteen minutes. I know—you don't have time. Neither do I. But an occasional stroll to the supermarket might give you some "down time" to think—or time to explore your neighborhood.

Bicycle. Some people go everywhere on bicycles. Those who live in cities may not consider this a safe means of transportation. Others live in a part of the country so vast that bicycles are not a viable option. Many people, though, live in places where a good bike (and helmet!) is an option.

Mass transit. Do you live in a metropolitan area that offers a safe alternative to car travel? When you consider how much it costs to operate your car, you may want to hop a bus. Also, lots of stop-and-go wears out a car *fast*.

Carpool. Some areas have designated express traffic lanes for carpool cars. Carpooling has lost some luster over the past few years, but is still a more sensible option than driving yourself.

Get Real. OK. Most of us simply cannot walk, bicycle, ride a bus, or carpool. *We need a car!* All right! What is the frugal thing to do?

BUY A NEW CAR?

This is a book about thrifty living, about saving money as best you can. You are not a felon if you go out and buy a new car. But logic tells us that buying a good used car is usually more sensible. Whether new or used, however, there are a few things you should know about buying a car.

For one thing, unless you live in a small town, you are likely to deal with more than one person at a car store:

- Salesman and his manager, who will estimate value.
- Finance manager, who will try to sell you financing. Car stores not only sell cars; a finance manager sells money, warranty, and credit life insurance.
- Accessories salesman (in a big dealership). This person sells floor mats, molding, bumpers, undercoating, stereo, etc. Forget the sticker in the window! All accessories are negotiable!

Caution. Puh-leeze! Learn this: When a dealer offers financing you may be offered money at a higher interest rate than you can find elsewhere. This caution applies to *any* situation where you are offered a contract with interest. What do I mean? In car sales, for instance, the finance manager buys money from a lending institution. He then sells the money to you. A typical sales pitch might sound like this:

Dealer: (who bought the money from a bank at 8 percent interest) "Can you afford $250 a month at 10 percent interest?"

Customer: (who cares only about monthly cost) "Yeah! I can handle that! Where do I sign?"

Wise consumers know this and will not let it happen. Shop for your own money or ask if the dealer is charging additional interest. There are times when dealers offer special low-interest rates that cannot be beat.

Rebates. A rebate is not a gimmick. It is financial help from the factory to help dealers move inventory—to "clear the lot."

"Cash Only." Although buying with cash is, indeed, the ideal method of purchase, many of us believe if we whisper a few magic words we get a better deal. This is rarely the case. These magic words have been passed from generation to generation like a treasured family recipe. We treat them as if they had real power, making *our* voices sound important and announcing: "I'm paying CASH." Think about this: When you sign a finance contract, what does the dealer do? He goes to the bank and *cashes* your contract. And gets a little kickback for writing the contract! There was a time when "cash" did work a little magic, but the spell fizzled long ago.

Trade in. Ever hear the promise of a $1,000 trade, as long as it has wheels? Tow it, push it, or carry it to the lot! This is a sales gimmick. All it means is that the dealer has at least $1,000 additional profit in a car. Go in and ask for the $1,000 discount without a trade. Leave the baby buggy home.

Best Bet: Does your car have value? You can save money if you do not trade but sell it yourself. Not many of us think we can do this. Which is why we *need* used-car salesmen! If you do sell the car yourself, beware of selling a used car to friends or relatives: If anything goes wrong, it can ruin a beautiful friendship!

Extended warranty. An extended warranty is a hedge against the future cost of labor and parts. It is also a gamble: Will your car need a new motor or transmission beyond the factory guarantee? Will repair costs skyrocket? If you bought an extended warranty and had to use it for a big-ticket item, you would certainly be glad! Good arguments can be made for and against this extra cost. Extended warranties on more modern cars can be a good buy because of complicated electronics, which are nearly impossible to repair at home.

Five-year plan. When I was little, a five-year plan was a farming method in the Soviet Union. Nowadays, it is an endless cycle that has sucked us in: Buy a car with next-to-nothing-down because you have no equity in your tired trade-in, opt for the barely affordable five-year plan, drive your new car down to its bolts until it has no value, trade it in because you have to, buy...

Listen: Long-term financing on a car is horrible! To get out from under this load, as Hank says, you have to "bite the bullet." Joe and I did. We sold our "new" car back to a dealer for what we owed (we were in the process of driving it down to its bolts), and now I drive the faithful little compact that got Joshua through high school and college. Eliminating the car payment and insurance cut a cool $300 from our monthly outgo. Yes, I am a bit embarrassed to drive the silly old thing, but that is far outweighed by the liberating feeling of a little step, one more step, out of the pit!

Insurance. The insurance that protects your car itself is called "physical damage." It consists of comprehensive coverage and collision coverage. Comprehensive covers most things that happen to a car outside of collision, with the exception of collision with an animal. Things such as fire, theft, vandalism, windshield chips and cracks, and animal collision are covered under comprehensive. Collision covers just that—your car banging into something: another car, a tree, a shopping cart in a parking lot. And hit-and-run damage when you are parked!

700. Always be sure to check with your insurance carrier about the physical damage rates on the car you are considering. It happened time and again when I was in the insurance business: Someone bought a used car that was highly rated for insurance... and the cost of physical damage insurance on the new "used" car was higher than the *newer* car it was replacing.

Physical damage rates are determined by such things as make, model, special features, horsepower, and the car's age. Let's use a brand new 1995 car as an example.

1995 (year 1) - Highest premium
1994-1993 (years 2 and 3) - Lower premium
1992-1991 (years 4 and 5) - Lower premium yet
1990 and before (year 6) - Lowest premium
Premiums level off and remain constant at year 6.

For instance, if you replace a small, newer compact with a slightly older luxury car, you will probably face higher auto premiums.

What should you do? If you want to buy a car, new or used, consider the following:

701. *Deal with someone who is reputable and honest.* Shop at an experienced dealership with a reputation for integrity.
702. *Be cautious—you may be a "number."* Some large car stores have highly trained sales staff and a refined system of selling cars. If you are in a store like this be on guard—you may no longer be a customer but a statistic. Salespeople rely on a rule of thumb that they will sell to three people out of ten.
703. *Decide the make and model car you would like.* Ahead of time.
704. *Research and establish the fair value of a car:* Check with a trusted mechanic, shop many dealers, read books and magazines. Once you have decided on a particular make and model, consult the famous "blue book" (found in your local library) for a general idea of value for that car.
705. *Buy quality, take good care of it, and it will last.* That seems to be a recurring theme from everyone.
706. *Search for a car that has a reputation for dependability.* Ask a trusted mechanic for an opinion.
707. *Consider mileage and overall condition.* However, don't be afraid of high mileage when looking at a model that is well-known for trouble-free, high-mileage performance.
708. *Ask about rebates,* how long the rebates are valid, and if they are expected to improve.
709. *Do not be unreasonable.* The car dealer is in business to make profit.
710. *Ask the salesman the final cost of the car.* Do not set yourself up for surprises after you have set sights on a car.
711. *Be a wise consumer.* Many dealers will avoid telling you the purchase price of the car, and will stick to comments such as "let's

talk about what you can afford." Have you ever been to one of these places? The salesman writes a figure on a piece of paper, folds it, slides it across the table as if you were negotiating World Peace, and makes his voice sound very serious: "Can you handle this?" Baloney! All that does is make you think you are participating in the decision! Stop that silliness! Don't be a statistic!

712. *Women customers—be informed!* I have spoken to several salesmen and mechanics about women. The most interesting response came from Jeff, a kind man who approaches women customers with the earnest intent to "tell her what she needs to know." Once Jeff realizes that the lady is well-informed and able to make an intelligent choice in such matters, he listens. Regrettably, women have helped perpetuate the myth that we know nothing about finances or anything with moving parts! Do your homework! If you are dealing with a character who will not respect you as a customer, go elsewhere.

713. *Get help if you need it.* For a set fee, a nonprofit consumer organization called "CarBargains" claims it can get your new car at significant savings. You tell them what you want; they shop the package. Call and ask for their brochure: 800-475-7283.

714. *There may be times when you have to settle for a rattle-trap because it is all you can afford.* Don't feel bad, and don't worry. Keep a good attitude and make a goal to take little steps toward affording "something better" next time... and if possible, go without until that "affordable something better" comes along.

715. *Why buy used?* Years ago, chances were you would buy someone's headache. In this disposable, replace-everything society we live in, many good used cars linger in lots.

716. *One big advantage of buying a used car:* You are buying a car on which someone has already taken the beating of depreciation. Depending on the make and model of the vehicle, a new car can reduce in value as much as $10,000 in the first year!

717. *Used cars have lower license fees, sales tax, and insurance.*

718. ***Patience is important in a used-car search.*** Know what you want and begin your search. Watch newspaper ads, car lots, auctions.

719. ***It is not always wise to buy a used car on the lot of a dealer selling that make.*** For instance, beware of buying a "Supergizmo" at the Supergizmo dealership. You will most likely pay top dollar because (1) the folks at Supergizmo Sales are convinced their cars are the best and (2) they have newer models for comparison. On Megamotors' lot, Supergizmo is just another used car.

720. ***On the other hand:*** Even though you might pay more for a Supergizmo at the Supergizmo lot, you improve your chance to get a good car. The previous owner may have upgraded. In other words: SHOP.

721. ***Credit unions historically offer lower interest but often require a higher down payment.***

722. ***Having good, clean credit will save you money.*** Lending agencies charge higher interest to people with poor credit.

723. ***Shop for the money yourself.***

724. ***Know thyself.*** Every person has a reason for trading. In our home it was the famous (or infamous) "nickel and dime" cliché. When miles added up and kinks came along, Joe would fret over being "nickeled and dimed to death." This is a valid concern. Yet it is worth wondering if nickels and dimes, after all, add up to less than big, fat dollars.

725. ***New or used: Do not buy on emotion!*** Do not fall in love with the car! Slow down! Do not run out and buy a car like a loaf of bread. Put thought into the process.

726. ***Speaking of emotion...*** Hank sends a strong tongue-in-cheek warning to all women: The love affair between a man and a car defies logic.

FOURTEEN

Drain Your Oil, Not Your Wallet

"You tell people they are car-poor," said Grim. And he is right. Aside from our home or our children's education, cars rank second in competition for our income. We invest an inordinate amount to own them. It is only logical that we care for them as best we can. Yet most of us have barely enough money to make payments, let alone repair or maintain a car properly. What happens when our maintenance dollar shrinks or disappears? Expensive breakdowns.

Use of cars. The last thing I want is to cause distress or give the impression that cars are a poor investment. Cars are absolutely necessary; very, very few of us can manage without one. Yet I had never confronted the actual cost of owning one before. I knew it was a neverending source of expense. But I had no idea how much of our hard work goes to maintain that hunk of steel grinning out in the garage! According to a booklet produced by the American Automobile Association (with data from Runzheimer International), there are average, national, per-mile costs to drive a car (see box).

Operating Costs:

This expense varies, depending on how you use your car. It includes gas, oil, maintenance, and tires.

Ownership Costs:

These are fixed costs that do not change, whether you drive your car or not. They include taxes, depreciation, finance charges, registration, insurance, and license fees. (Based on a four-year, 60,000-mile cycle; no youthful operator; pleasure use or to work less than ten miles.)

	Compact 1994 4 cyl	Sedan 1994 6 cyl	Luxury 1994 8 cyl
Per mile:	7.7 ¢	9.2 ¢	10.3 ¢
Ownership Costs:	$11.01/day	$12.56/day	$12.57/day

Total average cost per mile (including both operating and ownership costs)

	Compact	Sedan	Luxury
10,000 per year	39.8 ¢	46.6 ¢	58.4 ¢
15,000 per year	34.5 ¢	39.8 ¢	44.0 ¢
20,000 per year	31.2 ¢	35.7 ¢	39.3 ¢

Do it yourself—sometimes! There are many things you can learn to do, especially with older cars, but most repair on modern cars should be left to trained technicians. Modern cars come with sophisticated computers and electronic systems. Mechanics tell me many a car owner has moved a wire or a hose to save on repair bills only to face big bills later. You see, something happened about ten years ago:

Battalions of mechanics trained to twist a wrench were suddenly expected to wear white gloves and test vehicles by computer! Things are different now.

Do the basics yourself if you're certain you are not sabotaging the whole car. Check the manual that came with your car or call your dealer. If you are told to go ahead with do-it-yourself repair, remember the name of the person who advised you. *Caution:* Grandpa thought nothing of holding a spark plug to check the "juice." On today's cars that can be downright dangerous. Some cars have ignition systems that put out as much as 100,000 volts.

Jump start. My Uncle Gus had quite an assortment of cars. Jalopies would be a better term. Dear old Gus! He lived up the street from us. Many a time he would conscript the children in our neighborhood to push so he could get his car to start. I can still see us, pushing the car, with Gus behind the wheel. We would gather enough speed for the car to choke, sputter, and buck. Soon the engine would roar and Gus accelerated away as we fell on our faces in the road! Memories fill my mind of cold mornings when cars were routinely "jump started." It was a neighborly thing to do. From what I have learned it may no longer be the smartest thing to do. If someone asks you to "jump start" a car, check with your dealer first. Newer cars have delicate computer systems with low voltage: If you jump start someone, you may find yourself left behind with a mega-expensive computer repair.

Tire savvy. "Just because it's round and black doesn't mean it's the same," says Tom, my tire man.

All passenger car tires must conform to federal safety requirements for certain grades in tread wear, traction, and temperature. Every new tire has a label affixed which tells you the rating for the tire on all of the grades.

1. *Treadwear:* This grade is based on how the tire performed under controlled conditions in government testing. Figures can be a bit misleading because tires are normally run on a drum under con-

trolled conditions. Naturally, use of tire, rotation, and alignment will affect how well a tire wears, so grade is based on "average" or "normal" usage.

Here's how it works: Let's say the government decided the lowest possible grade for the controlled course is 100. If you buy a tire graded 200 that means it will wear twice as long as the tire graded 100. A tire rated 280 will usually get 20,000 to 30,000 miles. A tire rated 520 or above can be expected to get as much as 80,000 miles.

Consider mileage when spending money on tires. Also look for a dealer who is ready to stand behind the product. Tire warranties that "guarantee" that a tire will last beyond this treadwear rating may offer only limited protection. For example, if the tire wears out prior to the 50,000-mile warranty, a dealer might demand proof that your tires have been rotated every 5,000 miles. If you are able to do this, they may agree only to prorate the price of a *new* (overpriced) set of tires! Be sure to read the fine print.

2. *Traction:* From highest to lowest, traction grades are either A, B, or C. Traction means the tire's ability to stop on wet pavement under certain conditions. A is good; B is average; C may not have good traction. Tires with a treadwear rating of 100 to 400 are usually considered economy tires and do not provide the best traction.

3. *Temperature:* Temperature grades are A, B, and C, too. Remember that the faster you drive, the hotter your tires get. The temperature grade determines how well a tire will hold up to heat and how well it can dissipate heat. Sustained high temperature can reduce tire life or bring about sudden failure (blowouts!). The lowest level required to meet federal standards is C. A and B, of course, denote better quality.

This chapter is filled with advice to help break the breakdown syndrome. A little car savvy can help cut expenses in the long run.

$uper $avers

727. *Go to the head of the class.* If there are car-care courses in your area which instruct you on simple procedures, take one.

728. *"Tune-up" is becoming an old-fashioned term.* Many of us still think a poorly running car needs a tune-up. Today's cars are built to a standard of workmanship rarely seen before. In these days of new fuel injection engines, a running problem is probably related to a car's computer or emissions system.

729. *If your car does need a tune-up, you may be able to do it yourself.* In most cases all you need are new spark plugs and fuel filter. Be sure to check with the dealer! Also check in advance whether you will need special tools.

730. *Station savvy.* Go to the busiest gas station in town when you fuel up—less chance of water in the gas; often the best prices, too.

731. *Find a garage with a reputation for integrity and good work.* It's the best thing you can do for your pocketbook and your car. Develop a rapport with the mechanic. Do not do business with anyone who does not have "garage-keepers liability insurance."

732. *Pump your own!*

733. *Add a fuel additive every third tank of gas or so.* This keeps fuel clean. Dirty gas can cause one of your injectors to plug up, making your engine work harder. You may find a gasoline with a cleaning agent, but fuel additives can be bought cheaply from the gas station or automotive supply store.

734. *If you have an older model with a "history," you should check your oil every time you gas up.* Otherwise, check every other week or so and before you embark on a road trip. Do not add oil until the dipstick registers that you need to "add a quart." If your oil light comes on while driving, stop at once! Oil lights usually signal $$$BIG trouble$$$.

735. *Whatever you do, change your oil.* An oil change is a basic change you can master yourself. Everyone I have consulted is of the opinion that factory recommendations on when to change oil are too generous. We change oil every 2,500 miles, and are convinced this is a key element in avoiding expensive repair. If you do change your own oil, bring old oil to a service station with disposal facilities. Purchase the best brand oil and filter possible at the best price.

736. *What about the super-fast lubes?* As long as you are dealing with a reputable firm that is insured, this may be a sensible option. It depends on the price local independents charge for the same service. Keep in mind that these places often hire minimum-wage employees who may have minimal training.

737. *Don't be an "easy sell."* When the mechanic holds your dirty air filter under your nose and says, "Lady, this filter is filthy," say, "Why thank you for alerting me. I will tend to the matter promptly." Then buy one at a discount store—simple to install!

738. *Ditto windshield washer fluid* unless it's included with your service.

739. *Rotate your tires!!!* Every 5,000 to 10,000 miles. This is a money-saving tire tip. This is especially important if you have front-wheel drive which ruins front tires fast. Tire warranties demand proof you have rotated tires. Put the front on the back and back on the front. When you rotate, look for wear. This is the surest way to know if your car is out of alignment.
(Note: If you are a woman who has never changed a tire, I urge you to learn. It is not hard. Honest.)

740. *Alignment: the biggest killer of tires!* If your car is out of alignment you will go through new tires at an alarming rate. You will plead with the monkey-wrench bunch: "But I just *bought* those tires four months ago!" Make sure your car is in proper alignment.

741. *Brand name tires are not always the best quality.* Some off-brands have better tires that cost less.

Buyer beware! Don't be taken in by ads promising super sales. If tires are on sale, be sure mounting and balancing are included in the price. You should try to get an alignment included in the service, too. Ask for the "out-the-door" price before you purchase.

742. *Should you buy retreads?* My sources say no. You can buy an inexpensive radial for the same price and a radial tire is a good investment.

743. *Studded tires are helpful in climates that produce ice.* "Black ice" we call it here, and shudder when it is covering our highways! Studded tires and chains are banned in some states.

744. *Under-inflated tires cause greater wear and lower gas mileage.* The inflation level is stamped into the side of each tire. Check for proper inflation with your own pressure gauge.

745. *Silly as this sounds, take your car for a ride once a week.* One of the worst things you can do to a car is drive short distances without giving it a chance to roar down a highway. In short distances (under ten miles), your muffler does not get hot enough to burn off condensation. (For every four gallons of gas you burn you reap about one gallon of condensation.) And what does water do to metal? Yep… folks can hear you from a block away!

746. *Another reason to cruise once a week: If your car never warms enough to eliminate the products of combustion, the engine will sludge.* Ick. This leads to mechanical wear-down. You see, your engine creates acids. Something called the PCV system sucks the bad stuff out and burns it back in the engine. It takes time to purge the system. This is why traveling salesmen have great cars that go on forever; they are in constant operation. Cars like that.

747. *Unless the outside temperature is extremely cold, your car probably doesn't need time to warm up.* Anytime you start your car, however, drive easily for the first few miles. If cold and snowing, warm the car so the defroster can work properly.

748. *Did you know that a defroster runs the air conditioner in most new cars?* Don't be alarmed; it's good! This system must run periodically or it will lock up. Once you get the windows clear, just switch to your heater.

749. *Be sure your cooling system is in good working condition.* Ask the technician to quickly inspect it when it is in for service.

750. *Air conditioners cut gas mileage by about 2.5 miles per gallon.*

751. *Know your warranty rights!* By law there is no deductible on the warranty for your emission control system. A five-year, 50,000-mile warranty which is mandated by the federal government comes with every car regardless of the number of owners. A dealer makes more profit on a consumer repair than on warranty repair. Know your rights! Be sure you are not being wronged!

752. *Read your owner's manual and your warranty manual.* Any questions? There are 800 numbers for you to phone.

753. *If you replace your exhaust system (muffler), buy a lifetime system and keep your receipt.*

754. *Newer cars have brakes designed to "squeak" before you are in serious trouble.* The average life of front brakes is 40,000 to 50,000 miles, rear brakes 50,000 to 70,000 miles. Front brakes do 60 percent of the stopping. Once you hear a squeak have it checked. It may be nothing. If it is a sign of wear you will save bundles by servicing now.

755. *This is shocking.* Unless you are dealing with a trusted mechanic, be suspicious if anyone says you need shocks. My sources say this is one of the biggest waste areas in automotive care.

756. *Check your boots regularly! CV boots, that is.* Kirk and Jeff, brothers who operate a local shop, took me under a car to show me something called a CV boot. Most front-wheel or four-wheel-drive cars have boots. These are rubber "bellows" that protect the axle joints from dust and dirt. If the boot tears, the cost of replacing the axle is not far off. It is a *fix at once* proposition.

And it is not cheap. But the axle job costs much, much more. How can you tell if you need boots? Besides seeing the tear, once it has a hole or rip, grease will sling all around the area. Take a flashlight and slide under the front to check where the axle connects with the tire.

757. *Tried but true.* A paste of baking soda on battery terminals has removed corrosion.

758. *Kitty litter in the trunk is a must for winter travel.* If you get stuck, it provides terrific traction.

759. *Keep a shovel in the trunk for when you are stuck* in snow, sand, or mud.

760. *Cover windshield with plastic sheet during winter months* to keep frost from coating the windshield.

761. *Protect your dashboard from fading or cracking* with a cardboard shield.

FIFTEEN

Be Wise—Utilize! The Power of Conservation

Wanting to be more frugal with utilities, I devised a clothesline for our backyard. It consisted of hooks screwed into trees and lengths of rope with loops on each end. A sturdy birdhouse with a hinged top (thrift store) was nailed to a tree to hold clothespins and store the rope. Portable clothesline in seconds!

Is a clothesline a good way for you to save money? Yes! Clothes dryers use a lot of electricity. Does it take time to hang clothes? Yes. Do I always use the line? No. Sometimes I have no time. There are other drawbacks, too: Your husband may squeal; line-dried clothes are not soft! I found this out the hard way:

"This towel is rougher than a cob!" said Joe.

"Yes, dear, I know."

"I mean, feel it! Here!"

"Yes, dear, I know."

"I'm not used to drying myself with a scouring pad!"

"We all have to make sacrifices, dear."

The next week Joe added dryer sheets to my shopping list. Sigh. I wrapped them with red ribbon and stuck them in the "Isle of View" bag. Grim thought this was hilarious.

FLICK A SWITCH

Electricity, gas, phone, water, garbage: We use utilities daily, and we pay for that use, whether to a municipality, a corporation, a co-op, or a well-driller. It costs money with every turn of the faucet, flick of the switch, or toss of the trash. How can you save money? Easy! This chapter is filled with helpful information. You may be astonished at how easily you can reduce your use and your monthly bill.

Electricity. What do you know about electricity? Benjamin Franklin and Thomas Edison, right? Someone invented it, we can't live without it, it can be dangerous, and we get a bill at the end of the month. How is our monthly bill calculated? What costs the most to operate? How is energy used in our home?

Power is measured by how many kilowatts have been used over a specific period of time. One kilowatt-hour equals one kilowatt of power used for one hour. Here's how it works:

Suppose you have a 100-watt light bulb. If you use the light for five hours, you have used 500 watts of electricity. Since watts are a tiny amount of power, they are measured in "kilowatts." ("Kilo" means thousand.) Therefore, every thousand watts equals one kilowatt. Now, let's say you have four 100-watt bulbs that burn for five hours. You have used 2,000 watts, or two kilowatts. Get it?

Lighting consumes about 6 percent of an average home's energy costs. Electric companies charge per kilowatt hour (***kwh***). Want to know how much it costs to operate something? Read the print on it to determine how many watts it consumes. Multiply by the ***kwh*** rate shown on your power bill.

For the sake of illustration I will use a five-cent rate and my toaster, which uses 1,050 watts. 1,050 x 5 = 5,250. Point-off five places and we get .05250, or five and one-quarter cents per hour. Now let's say it is Thanksgiving, you are cooking on all burners and a turkey is in the oven. Figure an average full-range watt usage of

12,000, which equals 12 *kwh.* 12 x 5 equals about sixty cents per hour to cook your dinner.

Three kitchen appliances compete with each other for "most use of electricity in a single day." They are the stove, the refrigerator (especially auto-defrost types), and the chest freezer.

Three that share the title of "lowest use of electricity in a single day" are the clock, garbage disposal, and crockpot.

In your house, the heaters, air conditioner, and water heater are energy-consuming culprits, with your water bed and clothes dryer close behind. Three of the lowest users of power are the vacuum cleaner, sewing machine, and VCR.

All new appliances come with an EnergyGuide label. It tells you three things:

- Appliance type and capacity. Helps you compare appliances of similar size and with similar features.
- Estimated yearly energy costs. The lower the figure, the more efficient the appliance.
- Actual energy cost. This shows an assortment of "cost per year" figures based on different costs per kilowatt-hour.

Many of us worry about the energy consumption of air conditioners. As with all appliances, you must balance the factors of comfort and expense, and attempt to limit yourself to essential usage only. The average life of an air conditioner is twelve to fifteen years. The types of cooling systems are:

- Room air conditioners: mounted in windows and walls, to cool single rooms.
- Central air conditioners: to cool entire house through ducts.
- Heat pumps: similar to central air, but can "reverse" to provide heat in winter.

Gas. Depending on where you live, gas may be a sensible method to cut fuel or power cost. Gas is measured by BTUs, or thermal units. It takes 3,413 BTUs to equal one kilowatt-hour. Gas appliances usually cost less to operate, but you can buy a whole lot of kilowatt-hours for the price of investing in gas appliances!

762. *Call your electric company and ask the price per thermal unit of power.* Do the same with your gas company. Factor in cost of the heating device or appliance. Compare. It's that simple.

Oil. In some parts of our country it costs less to heat with oil. Whenever you compare costs for any type of power, however, consider maintenance and cleaning expenses as well as financial outlay when purchasing your heating unit.

INSULATE!

Insulation reduces drafts and keeps temperature constant. A single inch of standard insulation has the same effectiveness as forty-six inches of concrete! The most important areas to insulate are the attic, the floors, and the walls. A vapor barrier, on the "inside" side of some insulation, prevents condensation. Moisture damages insulation.

The effectiveness of insulation is measured in "R value": the higher the rating, the higher the insulating capability. According to an insulation professional, a good R value for cold climates is R 38 for ceilings and R 19 for walls. "Super Good Cents Homes," which are built for optimum insulation, normally have an R value of 49 for ceilings and R 26 for walls.

There are three types of insulation:

- Blanket, or batt: rolled-out fiberglass, already sized to fit between joists in the walls. This is usually the most economical.
- Rigid foam: sheets which can be cut to fit. This type gets pricey if you are trying to reach a higher R value.
- Loose fill: blown or poured through holes, usually at high cost because of the price of labor.

Windows. Up to 33 percent of a home's heat goes out windows and doors. It's well worth it to take energy-saving measures in the window department!

Storm windows and doors insulate by creating air space. Windows are rated by "U" value: The lower the rating, the better the efficiency, but the higher the price. Glass storm windows (in metal, vinyl, or wooden frames) are the most effective and the most durable. But you can devise your own storm windows from the following:

- Clear plastic, taped to the inside frame (neither durable nor long-lasting).
- Mylar (more durable, easier to see through).
- Rigid plastic, cut to fit the window.

Weather stripping and caulking. You can lose as much as 40 percent of your heat if your home is not weatherized; air leaks are among the largest sources of energy loss. The most common need for weather stripping is under a door. A quarter-inch gap at the bottom of your door could waste as much warm air as a three-inch hole in the side of your house!

763. ***Check for air leaks by holding a damp hand near an area.*** Close all doors and turn off fans when searching, concentrating on these problem areas:

around chimneys	recessed lighting
fireplace damper	electric boxes
ceiling fans	around doors and windows
attic access	around plumbing

Types of Weather Stripping

- Rolled vinyl with rigid metal backing: lasts longest; needs a good seal to be effective
- Foam rubber: short lifespan; easy to apply
- Thin spring metal: lasts well, but may lose sealing ability over time
- Rags and newspaper: a last resort!

Your utility company might offer rebates for weather stripping and caulking. When combined with weather stripping, caulking could save enough energy in the first year to pay for itself. Caulking is normally applied where two different materials meet, or where a space is evident.

Types of Caulking

- Expanding foam sealants: good for large cracks, but keep away from sun
- Backer rod or crack filler: flexible foam sold in long coils; use for large cracks or as backing for standard caulk

Caulk Ingredients

- Oil base: not very durable; least expensive
- Latex base: water soluble for use indoors; three to ten-year durability
- Butyl rubber: use outdoors, half-inch joints, three to ten-year durability; may take more than a week to cure
- Acrylic latex: for joints up to half-inch, indoors or out, durable; cannot be painted
- Elastomer: all applications; will not adhere to paint, cannot be painted, very durable

Passive solar energy. Some people invest in complicated systems of panels and pipes to collect solar energy. That can get expensive! But solar energy is not always costly. Want to use the sun? Get passive! Take advantage of the sun's heat in winter—or keep the sun away in summer. This is what we do:

The front of our home has a southwestern exposure, and is up a slight hill from an enormous lake. In summer it is impossible to sit on our deck—the rays are merciless. Awnings will not hold up to lake winds, so we invested in a gazebo-like sunscreen which we anchor to the main part of our deck, creating a "room" with shades that shield our western windows. We also close heavy blinds and windows to the west. It's a developing progression throughout the day; by late afternoon the western sun is most fierce. We do the opposite in winter, when sunshine is welcome during short days. Blinds are opened wide to greet any heat we can coax into this little cabin. You can do the same thing. Open or close drapes, blinds, or shades as you follow the sun throughout the day.

WATER

The National Rural Water Association says each person needs one hundred gallons of water every day.

Do you pay for water? If so, there are many ways to cut consumption *at no sacrifice in comfort to you!* For example, put a dent in dental hygiene:

According to the American Waterworks Association, if the tap is left running, the average person uses up to ten gallons of water while brushing teeth! Suppose you have a family of four and all brush teeth twice each day. That means ten gallons times eight toothbrushings wastes *eighty* gallons down the drain each day. That is the equivalent of 29,200 gallons each year. Let's say water costs 1.2 cents for each ten gallons. At that rate, you have pushed about $35 in cold cash down your sink drain.

Does your husband shave once each day? *Does he leave the hot water running?* Besides the cost of power to keep the water hot, do you know how much water he uses? On average, twenty gallons of hot water down the drain. That's twenty gallons down the drain each day, seventy-three thousand gallons a year, or $8.76 stuffed down the drain behind the toothbrushing money. That is over $40! You think I'm being nitpicky? Take two twenty-dollar bills and go flush them down the toilet. I dare you.

Instead, take the two twenty dollar bills and go out on the town—after he shaves.

You Can Save Water

(Data from the American Waterworks Association)

Activity	Normal Use	Conservative Use
Shower	Water running 25 gallons	Wet down, soap up with water off, rinse 4 gallons Use water restrictor
Tub bath	Full tub 36 gallons	Minimal water level 10 to 12 gallons
Dishwashing	Tap running 30 gallons	Use pan or sink 5 gallons
Automatic Dishwasher	Full cycle 16 gallons	Short cycle 7 gallons
Washing hands	Tap running 2 gallons	Fill basin 1 gallon
Toilet flushing	5 - 7 gallons	Use of tank displacement bottle 4 - 6 gallons
Washing machine	Full cycle, top water level 60 gallons	Short cycle, low water level 27 gallons

Drip, drip, drip. Leaky faucet? Sixty drops per minute loses 113 gallons per month, or 1,356 gallons each year.

764. Leaky toilet? A leaky toilet can break the budget! Check for leaks: Listen for the sound of running water Flush toilet Add yellow food coloring to the tank, wait ten minutes, then check the water inside the bowl. If you see color, ***fix at once!***

Keeping comfortable. Heating and cooling your home accounts for as much as 60 percent of your energy bill. Can you cut this cost without cutting comfort or investing in a new system? Absolutely, yes!

$uper $avers

765. ***The lowest comfortable thermostat setting means the greatest economy.*** But be careful: Do not become miserly with heat if you have young children or sick or elderly people in residence, or a computer. Perhaps you could keep a "warm room" to meet these needs.

766. ***Consider lowering your thermostats during the night.***

767. ***Be sure thermostats are not exposed to drafts;*** they should be on inside walls, away from windows and doors.

768. ***Learn to wear slippers and sweaters.*** Wear socks to bed like Grim!

769. ***Do not heat empty rooms*** unless there is plumbing there or you have a heat pump (the compressor can be damaged).

770. ***Keep closet doors shut!*** Why heat clothes in winter or cool them in summer?

771. ***Close the damper on your fireplace when not in use*** to save up to 8 percent of your heat. By the way, a fireplace adds about 12 percent heat to the average home, when in use.

772. ***In winter, use fans that ventilate to the outside sparingly.*** One hour of unnecessary operation can blow away a house-full of heated air!

773. ***Inspect heat pump or furnace and replace filters*** at least once each year.

774. ***Keep registers, baseboards, and radiators clean and clear of furniture or drapes.*** Air must circulate for maximum efficiency.

775. *Insulate heating system ducts and pipes.* Improperly sealed and uninsulated ducts can waste up to 25 percent of your system's heat.

776. *Install gaskets behind outlets to reduce heat loss.*

777. *Learn the "R" values for your area by calling a local lumberyard or insulation dealer.* Insulate accordingly.

778. *Wrap your water heater with insulation.* You can save up to 10 percent of water-heating costs. Check with your power company before you install insulation, especially if you have a gas hot water heater. This way, you will use the correct insulation, install it correctly, and be more likely to get an energy rebate.

779. *If installing insulation yourself, be sure you meet local codes and fire requirements.* Check with your utility company or a local lumberyard for instructions in safety and installation.

780. *Add a door sweep, a door "shoe," or a gasket threshold to stop door leaks.* Check with a hardware store or lumberyard for the easiest method for you.

781. *Find a caulk rated to stay flexible for twenty years.*

782. *Replace putty if missing around windowpanes.*

783. *Replace windowpanes if cracked.*

784. *If you have more windows than you can afford to cover with storm windows, begin with those that face north.* Then turn to the east or west. Do the south side last.

785. *Cut heat loss through doors by keeping traffic to a minimum!*

786. *Use natural ventilation in summer heat!* In the morning, open windows on the shady side of your house to let cool air in; keep shades drawn on the sunny side.

787. *In a two-story home, open first-floor windows on the shady side and second-floor windows on the sunny side*—cool air will force warmer air up and out.

788. *Use fans.* They cool inexpensively:

- For a small space set the fan to blow outside air in (provided it is cooler outside).

- For large areas, set the fan to push warm inside air out.
- Ceiling fans push cool air down across the floor and back up to the ceiling.
- Whole-house fans are usually installed in attics and can cool your house for less expense than central air conditioning.

789. *Do your baking early or late in the day* during hot months.
790. *Look for the SEER number on air conditioners.* Air conditioners are rated by "seasonal energy efficiency ratio" (SEER). The higher the SEER the better. Ratings of twelve or over are good.
791. *With an air conditioner, use "outside air" option only when necessary;* it costs less to recirculate cool inside air.
792. *Set it higher.* The higher the thermostat setting on an air conditioner, the less a machine will operate.
793. *Clean air conditioner filters monthly.*
794. *Clean condensers professionally every other year.*
795. *Try not to install a room air conditioner in direct sunlight.* North and east walls are best.
796. *Think small.* For small, well-insulated homes, individual room air conditioners are practical.
797. *Plant a leaf-bearing tree on your southwest exposure.* It will block direct sun during summer months, and without leaves in winter it lets the sun warm you. Plant evergreens on the north and west. These sturdy trees will protect your home from winter wind and cold.
798. *Wrap hot water pipes.*
799. *Repair leaky faucets!* Besides the monotonous drip, drip, drip, a water faucet leaking 60 drops a minute wastes 113 gallons of water a month. That's 1,356 gallons a year!
800. *Keep a bottle of water in the refrigerator* to avoid running the tap too long. Money down the drain.
801. *Cover your swimming pool when not using to prevent evaporation.* Do not fill it too high because of splash-out.
802. *Plant native outdoor plants that need less water.*
803. *Do not cut lawn short in hot weather.*
804. *Use drip irrigation and a water timer. Water your yard at night.*

805. *Consider low-consumption faucets.*

806. *Use a vegetable brush and short bursts of water* rather than letting your tap run.

807. *Use an electric razor for shaving.* If you and hubby become accustomed to an electric shave you will save water, blades, shave cream, razors, and the cost to heat water. It's worth a try!

808. *Take showers instead of baths.* They usually require half as much hot water. Remember! After five minutes a shower becomes recreation.

809. *Trying to be frugal? Take five-minute showers!*

810. *Install a low-flow shower head: twenty gallons saved every five minutes.* Faucet aerators and efficient showerheads mean big savings! Some power and water companies supply showerheads free.

811. *Use the sink stopper.* Do not let hot water run down the drain while shaving or washing dishes!

812. *Always use cold water in garbage disposals.*

813. *Feed garbage scraps to animals or use as compost* to reduce use of garbage grinder.

814. *Use cold water for washing clothes whenever possible.*

815. *Reduce the amount of flush water* by filling and sealing two plastic, one-quart bottles with sand or rocks and placing them in the tank, *away from the flushing mechanism.* Do not use bricks; they damage your mechanism.

816. *Turn off your water heater.* If your home is unoccupied for more than three days and your water heater is protected from freezing, turn it off.

817. *Clean sediment buildup* in water heater to help efficiency.

818. *Wash your car with short bursts from hose.* Wash it near a hedge or shrub so the plant benefits from a free drink. Residual soap will act as insect repellent for the plants.

819. ***For more advice on water consumption write:*** The National Rural Water Association, P.O. Box 1428, 2915 S. 13th, Duncan, OK 73534.

820. ***Consider fluorescent lighting.*** Standard incandescent bulbs are big energy wasters, losing as much as 90 percent of energy as heat. They also wear out quickly. Fluorescent bulbs use about one-fourth as much energy and last as much as ten times longer. If you are using an incandescent light more than two hours each day, switch to a compact fluorescent bulb.

821. ***Turn off lights in unoccupied rooms.***

822. ***Take advantage of sunlight whenever possible.***

823. ***Reduce background light and use "task lighting"*** for such things as reading.

824. ***Clean light bulbs and fixtures*** and improve efficiency by 100 percent!

825. ***Use dimmer switches when possible.***

826. ***If a fixture uses several bulbs, use one higher-wattage bulb rather than several small ones,*** but never exceed the fixture's recommended UL bulb size.

827. ***Use fixtures with three-way switches.***

828. ***Make your home energy efficient with lighter colors.*** Dark colors absorb light.

829. ***Use reflectors in light fixtures.*** They can double the amount of light.

830. ***Use outdoor lights only when needed.***

831. ***Side-by-side refrigerator-freezers use more energy than same-sized top-freezer units.***

832. ***Manual defrost models use half as much energy as automatic-defrost refrigerator-freezers,*** but they must be defrosted regularly.

833. ***Avoid automatic ice-makers and dispensers.*** They increase energy consumption.

834. *Keep your refrigerator and freezer temperatures adjusted.* Refrigerator temperatures should be 36°F-38°F; a freezer should be 0°F-5°F. As little as ten degrees below what is recommended can increase energy use by 25 percent.

835. *Keep refrigerator and freezer as full as possible,* but be sure doors close tightly and air circulates freely.

836. *Clean condenser coil* under or behind refrigerator a couple of times each year.

837. *Open refrigerator doors as seldom as possible.* I think ahead and try to take all ingredients out at once; same when returning.

838. *Cool cooked foods before placing in refrigerator.* Grim cools—and sometimes freezes!—food in the snow.

839. *Do not put uncovered liquids in the refrigerator.* They emit vapors that cause condensers to work harder.

840. *Avoid situating freezers and refrigerators in cold areas* such as porches or garages. They do not operate efficiently in such environments.

841. *Thaw frozen foods in the refrigerator.* This adds cold, and is much safer when thawing meat.

842. *Match pots and pans to diameter of the heating unit.* A small pot on a big burner equals wasted energy. A big pot on a small burner uses more energy.

843. *Cook with pans that have clean, flat bottoms.*

844. *Use as little water as possible when cooking.* Better nutrition, better flavor, better energy consumption.

845. *Keep reflector pans clean on your stovetop.*

846. *If using an electric stove, turn off the elements several minutes before the allotted cooking time.*

847. *If using a gas stove, check your flame.* The color should be blue for maximum efficiency. If yellow, the burner may be clogged with food particles. Clean it with a pipe cleaner.

848. *Thaw food before cooking.* A frozen roast requires as much as 50 percent more cooking time.

849. *Do not open the oven while baking or roasting!* A sneak preview can cause the temperature to drop twenty-five degrees.

850. *Maximize your oven use.* I rarely heat my oven without cooking at least one more item.

851. *If using the self-cleaning oven feature, do so after regular oven use.* The heat is already halfway there.

852. *Self-cleaning ovens use less energy for cooking* because of extra insulation.

853. *Leave the door ajar when the oven is turned off for added heat in winter* (but never use the oven to heat your kitchen!).

854. *When purchasing a gas range, consider an electronic ignition system instead of a pilot light,* which is always burning and using gas. However, be aware that the igniter must be replaced periodically, an added expense.

855. *Convection ovens use about one-third less energy than conventional ones.*

856. *Use microwaves, toaster ovens, and pressure cookers for small meals*—for a fraction of the cost.

857. *Keep the lid on!* You will cook faster at lower temperatures.

858. *Heat only the amount of water you need for a cup of tea.* The microwave is your best choice.

859. *Use glass or ceramic oven pans.* They require about twenty-five degrees less heat than metal.

860. *Dishwashers that use less water use less energy.* Water heating accounts for 80 percent of a dishwasher's energy use.

861. *If your dishwasher has a temperature "booster," reduce your water heater setting to 120-130° F.* Most people keep their hot water temperature high because of the dishwasher. You might not need to.

862. *Use the "light" wash setting, if possible, and "no-heat" drying.* Your dishes will still be clean.

863. *Operate with a full load.* Saves running the dishwasher often.

864. *Scrape excess food first.* I know, some dishwashers claim you don't have to. With most, though, you do! Otherwise debris will enter the pump and meddle with efficiency.

865. *Check the filter screen over the drain regularly.* Remove food particles, silverware, plastic lids, chopsticks, etc.

866. *Turn off dishwasher entirely when dry cycle begins.* This will save power and add humidity to your home. Open door to air dry.

867. *Do not use the dishwasher to warm plates.* Use leftover oven heat.

868. *Do not run the dishwasher when someone is taking a shower:* balance hot-water demand.

869. *Follow detergent instructions for both dishwasher detergent and clothes-washer detergent.*

870. *Wash full loads of clothes unless you can regulate settings.*

871. *Do not overwash clothes;* delicates, for instance, use a short cycle.

872. *Use hot water only when necessary;* it accounts for 90 percent of a washer's energy consumption.

873. *Use cold water rinse when possible.*

874. *Check the washing machine lint filter often.* Anything that slows down efficiency causes any appliance to use more power.

875. *Use front-loading machines:* They use one-third less water.

876. *Use a dryer with an automatic shut-off.* They save upwards of 15 percent over dryers with timers.

877. *Operate your dryer with a full load* (not crammed).

878. *Load your dryer with fabrics of similar weight* (e.g., do not dry jeans with shirts).

879. *Keep the lint filter clean on your dryer.*

880. *Vent the dryer to increase efficiency.* Be sure your vent is not clogged.

881. *Try to keep your dryer in a warm area.*

882. *Remove dried clothes promptly.* Grim irons with his hands by smoothing and folding clothes straight from the dryer.

883. *Use a clothesline whenever possible.* Does it take time to hang clothes? Yes. Do I always use the line? No. Sometimes I have no time.

884. *Turn off TV, radio, stereo, when not in use.*

885. *Try to towel-dry your hair before using hair dryer.*

886. *Cover water beds with comforters for insulation.*

887. *Do not overload your food disposal.*

888. *Use small electric appliances such as fry pans* instead of your stove.

889. *Turn off appliances when not needed.* Is your coffeepot still on from this morning? Are you making sludge? Turn it off!

Home energy audit. Remember the concept of ownership? Get your family involved! Turn this into an energy audit week, followed by a family meeting over tacos or pizza. Ask your local utility if a representative will visit (without charge) to help with energy-saving tips. Build your family meeting around that visit. Display utility bills; talk about your monthly payments. Prowl around the house, inside and out. Look for places where weather stripping and caulking could do some serious good. Check all faucets. Read your electric meter every night for a week and discover which day consumed the most energy. Figure out why. Help the kids develop math skills by determining how much electricity all of your small appliances use. Use coins to demonstrate cost or projected savings. Award a prize to the child who conserved the most energy during the week.

COMMUNICATIONS

Telephone. Because telecommunications technology is changing rapidly, it is impossible to make general statements about phone rates. Calling patterns differ from one person to the next, there is an assortment of local phone companies, and competing long-distance firms make this a complicated issue.

Cellular phones. "Cell" phones have advanced greatly since the days of "breaker, breaker, good buddy" citizen's band radios. From CB popularity and demand came the development of more frequency space and spectrum and the creation of lots of air time.

Many people like the convenience, safety, and reliability of carrying a portable phone with them wherever they travel. There is nothing economical about a cell phone. Consider the cost of buying your cell phone, along with the monthly operations cost, and the cost when you move into other cell "territories." Go into this kind of proposition well-informed to prevent surprise bills from popping up at the end of the month.

Pagers. Some other services are less expensive than cellular phones. Although technology has been with us a long time, one-way communications are experiencing a sudden popularity.

Pagers are increasingly popular, partly because they are economical. Pagers come with an audio or a visual function, and can be as small as a pencil or a wristwatch. Messages will come to you as long as you roam within a particular area. The visual version scrolls messages across a small screen on units as small as a box of matches. Pagers are excellent tools for babysitters or for parents with teens, since they are a means of immediate contact. Pagers can be purchased at discount stores, from the paging service itself, or they can be rented.

One paging firm rents out a "baby beeper" for the last few months of pregnancy. Dad wears the beeper and Mom can contact him—through the paging service—when the blessed time comes. Or when she's in the mood for ice cream! Here are some money-saving tips in the communications department:

$uper $avers

890. *Study your family's calling pattern.* Ask the customer service department of local carriers to customize a program to fit your needs; compare results and sign with the best program.

891. *Forget advertisements:* Look closely at each carrier to see if their services suit you. All carriers charge different rates; know your prices!

892. *Mail a copy of your last bill to prospective carriers* and ask for suggestions.

893. *Know when long-distance rates are cheapest:* (weekends, holidays, after business hours.)

894. *Use a timer to limit your long-distance calls!*

895. *Dial direct.* Do not use the operator for assistance unless necessary.

896. *Try to obtain 800 numbers for businesses you must call.* The simplest method is to call 1-800-555-1212 and ask for a listing. If none, call the business (during your cheap-rate time if in another time zone) and ask the business for its 800 number. If none, leave your number and ask that a service representative call you back.

897. *Write letters.* They're less expensive than phone calls.

898. *Plan what you will say before you call,* unless you have unlimited local service. Make a list!

899. *If you like to talk on the phone, rustle up a willing ear in your exchange (if you have unlimited local calls) and talk away.* You will get it out of your system and save the cost of a long-distance call.

RECYCLE, PRECYCLE

Gary runs our county landfill and teaches a class about waste management. I expected him to tell me how people could reduce disposable trash: recycle, compost, crush cans. Gary agreed that recycling is a good thing to do. It takes 95 percent less energy to remanufacture something. Aluminum cans and glass, in particular, can be turned into useable products.

As a matter of fact, what we call "waste" becomes another country's natural resource. We send battalions of container ships abroad, carrying our paper and plastic for other countries to use as raw material. Some of that paper is shipped back to us as recycled paper—a long round trip. But Gary seemed to have something else on his mind. He introduced me to the new word in garbage: PREcycling. Never mind what you are going to do with it, insisted Gary, don't have it in the first place!

Precycling. Want to save money on your garbage bill? Start by auditing your shopping cart. What do I mean? Consider an individual lunch-box-sized serving of chocolate cake:

- You are paying much more for the individually wrapped serving.
- You are spending your money on junk food that has no redeemable food quality.
- You are creating potential litter; do your taxes pay for street cleanup?
- You are creating garbage to go to your local landfill; do your taxes pay for landfill maintenance?

Who pays? For one thing, we all pay for garbage, one way or another. Whether it is in water, air, or land quality; through taxes that keep our landfills running; or through monthly refuse collection fees; we all pay. But is there a way to cut back on how much you pay? Depends on how you are billed. *(1) By weight:* In some places, refuse is weighed by computer. A computer chip is installed in your refuse bin and scanned as it is brought alongside the truck. You are billed by weight. In this case, you can save by reducing your overall refuse. Also, some landfills charge individuals by poundage. *(2) By volume:* This is probably the most common method of determining your fee.

You pay a monthly fee for a certain number of cans, bins, or pails. If you can cut back on garbage, you might reduce your bill.

Joe and I have been recycling for years. Sometimes we drop our assorted cans, glass, cardboard, and paper into community bins. When time allows, we haul our collection to a recycling firm and get paid for the stuff. We use an old grape-jelly jar as a special bank to hold our recycling income: Money we save for our future grandchildren.

$uper $avers

900. *Precycle newspapers:* Do you receive more than one paper? Why? Can you read your paper during a break at work, at a nearby library? Can you share a paper with a neighbor? Can you satisfy your need-to-know by watching the evening news or by listening to the radio?
901. *Precycle pop and juice containers:* Drink water.
902. *Precycle anything made microwave-ready:* Do not buy.
903. *Precycle much in your grocery cart:* Buy bulk; bring your own containers if possible. If not, use paper bags and reuse them for lunch containers.
904. *Save money by buying smart (see food chapter), and reduce waste as a bonus!* Write on an index card: *Shopping cart = Garbage pail.* Tape that to the handle of your cart next time you shop.
905. *Precycle food leftovers: Make a compost pile.* What if you live in a high rise? Use a bucket on the terrace or fire escape or get a neighborhood compost pile going.
906. *Analyze the contents of your garbage pail to figure how to slash your trash.*
907. *Get off mailing lists!* Paper products account for 40 percent of our refuse. If tired of filling your pail with mail, write to:

     Mail Preference Service
     c/o Direct Marketing Association
     P.O. Box 9008
     Farmington, NY 11735-9008

SIXTEEN

Pet Pourri

Why this fascination—this bond—that we have with pets? After all, they are costly, demanding, and time-consuming. They smell, create chaos, and get us into trouble. They poop, get under our feet, and they die.

Have you ever looked into the big brown eyes of a Labrador retriever? Eyes directed at you? Eyes that say, "Hey, I know you're busy, but just one touch of your hand will do. You know my favorite spot. Just a little tickle. Then I'll lie down at your feet and guard you. I love you." That's why.

WHERE TO GET A PET

If you are trying to be frugal, do not buy a pet from a store or a breeder. Go to the pound. An adoption fee is significantly less than the cost of pedigree. Many shelters have arrangements with veterinarians and credit part of your fee toward medical or neutering cost.

A pound of trouble? Are you adopting someone's headache? Maybe. Undisciplined pets soon become a nuisance for improperly trained owners, and the dog pound is too convenient a dumping ground for unmanageable animals. We, however, have four-legged critters lying on our floor that prove that quality animals can be found at the pound: Teddy (aging cocker), Cinder (older Labrador),

Madison (older grey cat), and Snipe (striped cat). Drake (Joshua's Lab) came from a private home to replace our beloved Jacob (Lab puppy from pound) who was killed.

I know. You are thinking this isn't frugal at all. You are right! So stay away from the pound if you have a soft spot like we have.

Picking a dog. Take your time. Borrow books, magazines, or videos from the library. Study and decide as a family what kind of animal you would like. Look for breeds to suit your lifestyle: There are animals that don't bark, don't shed, do love children, don't love children, love the indoors, love the outdoors, love water, are easy to train, are hard to train, are overprotective—or would welcome an intruder with tea. Call your local shelter and ask them to call if the breed you want comes their way. Also watch classified ads.

High Maintenance Breeds	Low Maintenance Breeds
Shar Pei	Golden Retriever
Cocker Spaniel	Labrador Retriever
Bichon	Beagle
Poodle	
Afghan	
Chow	

Adopt a healthy adult animal that has already been:

- neutered
- immunized
- housebroken
- disciplined and obedience-trained
- heartbroken and in need of your loving touch

Whether you have a family or are a single person, consider spending time at the local shelter before you get a pet. Walk puppies, water dogs, clean cat cages. There is no better way to drill home responsibility than to witness tragic failures. (And if you do this, I guarantee that all your plans for a "perfect" dog or cat will disappear when a homeless critter adopts you! You will disintegrate into a hopeless heap and bring it home.)

If it's not broken, fix it! "Fix" your pets! Get them neutered or spayed as soon as possible. If you happen to want your children to witness the miracle of birth, rent a video from the library.

Yes, puppies and kittens are cute. Unwanted ones, and those that find their way into the wrong hands, are also battered, maimed, abandoned, killed, beaten, abused, and starved. If you cannot afford the neuter fee, you may find aid at the Humane Society. Or talk with veterinarians until you find one who will cooperate with your budget.

Immunize! Prevention is key: Immunize! If you cannot afford immunization, do not get the animal. Cats and dogs are subject to an assortment of deadly diseases. Should your pet battle one, the fees for medical care can be astronomical.

Be absolutely certain to follow the immunization schedule. Animal immunization targets certain ages at certain intervals (e.g., canine parvo must be given up to the first twenty weeks of life to be preventive).

Immunizations–Dogs

- Canine distemper: widespread, often fatal
- Canine adenovirus 1 and 2: infectious hepatitis, respiratory infection; can result in kidney damage
- Canine leptospirosis: bacterial infection; spreads to other pets and humans
- Canine parainfluenza: respiratory infection
- Canine coronavirus: highly contagious intestinal disease
- Canine parvovirus: highly contagious intestinal disease
- Rabies: almost always fatal, transmitted to humans through bites

Immunizations–Cats

- Feline distemper: widespread, contagious, high death loss
- Feline viral rhinotracheitis: highly contagious respiratory disease
- Feline calicivirus: serious respiratory infection
- Feline pneumonitis: respiratory ailment caused by an organism, chlamydia
- Rabies: almost always fatal

CARE AND GROOMING

Evaluate your situation before you get a household pet. Can you afford to feed it, keep it healthy, license it, and invest your time? You should be able to spend at least fifteen minutes each day with your pet. If you cannot make the commitment, get a goldfish.

A little common sense goes a long way in the pet care department. Do you want a long-haired pet? You will need to brush it every day. Or consider investing in an electric shaver with attachments to shave your long-haired dog—after proper instruction. If you don't want to do either, then don't acquire a long-haired pet.

Never leave a dog in your car on hot days. Ever. Also, do not let your dog ride in the back of a pickup truck unless the dog is safe from falling or jumping out. If it is tied up while riding, make sure it cannot hang itself or jump and be dragged.

Invest in a plastic-coated cable with which to tie up your dog when necessary. Oh. So you wouldn't tie up a dog? Would you rather scoop him up off the street? Oh. So *your* dog would never roam, especially if you're at home? We scooped up Jacob off a highway a couple of years ago. Up until that time he had never left our property.

Consider these additional hints, which combine prudent care with the desire to save money:

$uper $avers

908. *We buy puppy food from a warehouse store.* Puppies need special food because of bone formation.

909. *Our animals get along well on moderately priced kibble.* Some people prefer higher-priced food for pets because animal waste is reduced.

910. *We do not buy the cheapest food and we do not switch from one brand to another.* We watch newspaper ads and buy dog food when it is on sale, always with a money-off coupon.

911. *My vet, Debbie, advises against feeding generic brands; they are not properly formulated.* Feeding the wrong food can result in hair loss, weight loss, and poor skin.

912. *We do not give canned food unless the weather is extremely cold* and we want to fortify our animals with extra nutrition.

913. *Because our cats spend nearly all their time outside, we reduce their food during summer* when they munch on bugs. Note: If your cat eats varmints outdoors, check with your vet. The cat should be wormed each year.

914. *We feed scraps to our animals.* If you do, you will learn fast what foods your pets can't handle. We never give a big dose of fat, although we add a little oil to their food. They are in egg-yolk heaven when I'm on a no-fat kick! But my vet does not recommend feeding scraps.

915. *A big knuckle bone (after stock-making), is like a Hershey bar to a dog.* Take away any bone showing splinter potential. Debbie also reminds us that they are really bad on lawnmowers!

916. *Find logical alternatives to "special" food.* Joe and I lingered in the pet food aisle one day trying to find something to feed Teddy, whose teeth are grinding down. "Special diet" food was expensive. Joe suddenly muttered, "How dumb are we?!" Do you need to soften the crunch for an old-timer? Add water.

917. *Offer to buy damaged packages at a bargain.* Ask your grocer if a ripped sack of pet food sits in the back room.

918. *Measure!* If you do, you will be surprised how far a sack of food will go. Once you know the minimum your pet can thrive on, stick to that. Many of us are guilty of overfeeding our animals. Some of us shower them with so much attention, Debbie says, that we turn our pets into "small hairy children." When you overfeed, you are hurting your pet and you are hurting your pocketbook. I also believe you are hurting the heart of a holy God when there are children fed less than your spaniel.

919. *Do you give your pet vitamins?! Why?* I love my pets, too, but I sure think the Lord would rather I put money saved from pet "frills" toward feeding needy human beings!

920. *Call different vets and compare prices for services* such as immunizations. The average cost for an entire immunization series for a young dog is $100.

921. *Dry pet shampoo: baby powder rubbed in, then brushed out.*

922. *Cheap pet bath: Bring pet to a lake or stream.* Do not do this with an animal that fears water.

923. *Don't buy expensive kitty litter!* Stop and think about what that stuff is used for. Why spend extra money for *that!* Has Madison Avenue dulled your senses? Buy the cheapest you can get, keep it clean and sprinkle it with baking soda.

924. *Emergency kitty litter—shredded newspaper.*

925. *Old leather belts make good collars when cut to size.*

SEVENTEEN

How Does Your Garden Grow?

"Six years you shall sow your field... but during the seventh year the land shall have a sabbath rest" (Lv 25:3-4). Who better to teach us about ecology than the Creator of the land? He certainly uses lots of gardening terms throughout His Word: pruning, planting, toiling, harvesting.

The Bible has clear instruction to properly care for our land, and I believe it pleases God when we lovingly cultivate crops. Are you thinking about a harvest of your own? Would you like to plant a garden and watch it grow? You may need some friendly advice before you grab your hoe!

Ever wondered why Mary Mary was "quite contrary"? I have it figured out: weeds. You see, she jumped into her garden project with great enthusiasm. She dug up the backyard, bought truckloads of young plants from the nursery, donned special cap and gloves, and set out to become a veritable vegetable valedictorian. "Wailing weed woman" was probably more like it. She was despondent. What did she do wrong?

Maybe you're still smarting from your last brush with nature. Determined to eat wholesome, organic produce, or to economize, you also may have come home with a truckload of plants and tried to grow a garden. You put time and effort into your undertaking; sincerely intending to grow your own. Whether in containers on the deck or in a patch of yard, it started out great, didn't it? Until you didn't keep up and it was out of control. Until bugs dropped by for brunch. Until you tired of dirty fingernails. Determination turned to disappointment; disappointment to guilt. Time and money wasted, you looked the other way when you passed the jungle of dandelions crowding your squash.

Don't let past failures stop you! If you are intent on farming, start small: Plant a salad! Plant a few containers or a small plot with lettuce, tomatoes, radishes, and parsley. Plant some colorful (and edible!) nasturtiums. If successful, add cucumbers next year.

Look before you leap. Gardens are not for everyone. For someone like Linda, grand grower of pumpkins and assorted produce, gardening is therapeutic. For others it is more like a pain in the neck. All things considered, getting into the garden business can be expensive! Whoa! Isn't it much *cheaper* to grow your own food? Not necessarily. A garden is a big project that requires planning, money, and time. Remember—planting is the easiest part of gardening!

Easy to Grow
bush beans
carrots
cucumbers
lettuce
radishes
squash

Quick-Growing
radishes
lettuce
spinach
summer squash
Swiss chard

Good for Containers
cherry tomatoes
herbs
lettuce
squash

Good for Small Spaces
tomatoes
snap beans
lettuce

And there is more: What will you do with the food you grow? It has to be eaten promptly—or stored. Produce does not wait for you to be "in the mood." Whether free, homegrown, or store-bought, it must be processed in a short time or it becomes waste. To store the food you may need a root cellar, a freezer, a dehydrator, or a canner. To can you need jars and lids. All of the food preparation takes time. Consider the cost of everything!

Or cut corners as I do: Have a friend who loves to garden. I help Jim deal with excess food: I take it off his hands. This is a nice arrangement—no waste for Jim, my cupboards and freezers are full!

$uper $avers

926. *Your project should begin at the library.* Borrow books on gardening. There is a vast selection of manuals to guide you.

927. *Talk to people who garden.* Seek advice; learn from others. There is no better teacher than experience.

928. *Whenever you have gardening questions, call the county extension agent for answers.* Every area has one, and the service is free.

929. *Plan your garden.* Sketch your plan and think the process through.

930. *If buying stock from a nursery ask about the plants*—where they came from, if they have been outside, if they are "local" (and therefore heartier).

931. *Know your prices!*

932. *Wait until greenhouse prices drop* before you rush out for that truckload.

933. *Buy a six-pack for less than one big, mature plant.* The big guy was little once, too!

934. *Best bet: Start plants from seeds yourself.* It is to your advantage if you start your seeds in the ground. Ground-started seeds do not face transplant shock, are easier to plant, and are cheaper than nursery plants. But begin seeds indoors if the outdoor growing season is short.

935. *Use egg cartons or old plastic or foam cups to start seeds.*

936. *Purchase a good starter mix for the seeds, but it need not be a name brand.*

937. *Do not start more plants than your family can use.* If a seed packet yields more than you need, share it with a friend. Each of you start a different pack of seeds, splitting the results for planting.

938. *Start a garden co-op with friends.* Each assumes responsibility for a certain "crop." Key word: responsibility.

939. *Don't always make a long, skinny row, one seed wide.* Sometimes you can make wide rows of seeds side by side for a greater yield. This also lets you plant lots in a small area.

940. *Keep ground wet until the seeds germinate. Then don't water as often.* Linda insists that after crucial germination gardens need very little water. If we pour on the water, roots stay shallow because their supply is on the surface. If water is withheld, roots will dive into the ground looking for a drink. This makes a much better plant. Do not water a droopy plant after intense sun. If it's droopy, water only in the morning. Soak the ground thoroughly.

    Some plants have better flavor with less water: corn, carrots, squash, pumpkin, tomatoes. The potato needs little water to grow.

941. *Hoe! Hoe! Hoe!* Weeds use up fertilizer, nitrogen, and water: everything you are trying to get to your plant! If you see green where it is not supposed to be, you have trouble. Hoe, rake, or pull weeds. Put them in a bucket and haul them away. Also, plant right after soil is worked. If you till the ground one weekend and plant the next, guess what gets a head start on your vegies? Yep. Weeds.

942. *Layers of newspaper covered with dry grass clippings hold down weeds and decay into mulch.* Skip the black plastic: It is used to attract the sun due to its dark color. Dirt, however, is dark

enough already. Plastic can prevent water from getting into the ground, is an extra expense, is slippery, and must be disposed of.

943. *Fertilize frugally.* Use moderation in all you do.

944. *Remove plant waste, except peas.* Most plants will rob soil of nitrogen when turned back into the soil; peas are an exception.

945. *Create your own compost with kitchen scraps* (no meat or oil).

946. *Be careful with animal waste*—it can burn your plants. Try to buy sterilized manure so you don't sow seeds from every weed the cow munched.

947. *Use an old, labeled saltshaker to sprinkle fertilizer alongside the plants.* Do this when seeds first germinate, once during growth, and just as the fruit begins to set.

948. *Plant compatibly.* Marigolds are an old standby for organic gardeners: The smell keeps many bugs away.

949. *Avoid extra-buggy plants* like those in the cabbage family. I once grew the wormiest broccoli in history!

950. *Repel aphids* and other light-winged insects with dish detergent diluted in water, with a good soapy feel.

EIGHTEEN

"Paper or Plastic?"

How many times have you heard that little query? And what was your answer? Since 40 percent of landfills are filled with paper, should you opt for plastic? And what do you do with your bag collection?

For one thing, whether you cart your groceries home in paper or plastic, you can always bring your sacks back the next time you shop. Or you can do what I do: I have a couple of mesh bags that stretch to unbelievable proportions in which to haul home my purchases. Since I am careful to precycle and audit my cart, my grocery load is small to begin with. What else can you do with all those bags? Can you reuse old magazines, other paper products? Is "disposable" a dirty word?

TEN USES FOR PAPER BAGS

951. *Wrapping paper*—for gifts or for packages to be mailed.

952. *Containers.*

953. *Better than paper towels for blotting greasy food!*

954. *Children's crafts.*

955. *Cooking.* Bake a turkey inside. Line a cookie sheet when making meringues.

956. *Luminarias.* Cut designs on the sides, fill the bottom with dirt, put lighted candles inside to line walkway during holiday seasons or on special summer nights.

957. *Small surface protection* when painting small items or cleaning fish.
958. *Emergency cutting board.*
959. *Garbage can liner.* Also, fold one in thirds and put on bottom of garbage can, under the bag for added protection.
960. *"Shake and bake" coating shakers for chicken and fish.*

TEN USES FOR PLASTIC BAGS

961. *Line garbage pails* (or paper sacks used for garbage).
962. *Additional wrapping for freezer storage.*
963. *Wet clothes "hamper,"* or to haul wet clothes or towels.
964. *Emergency rubber gloves.*
965. *Emergency rain hat or shower cap.*
966. *"Scarecrow" in your garden.* Let it flap in the breeze.
967. *Shipping protection in place of other padding.*
968. *Christmas decoration storage.*
969. *Litter bag in your car.*

TEN THINGS TO DO WITH OLD MAGAZINES

970. *Use them to make homemade greeting cards.*
971. *Donate them to a retirement home or a hospital or a library.*
972. *Use magazine pages to wrap small presents.*
973. *Use them for children's school projects or crafts.*
974. *Use them as a "floor" in garbage sacks.*
975. *Frame nice covers using inexpensive frames.*
976. *Use crumbled pages for packing material.*

977. *Wind Christmas lights around rolled-up magazines.* No more tangles!

978. *Share them with friends.* Key word: return.

979. *Give them as gifts.* I do this: I subscribe to one favorite magazine for pleasure. I save a year's supply and present it as a Christmas gift to a person with similar interest.

980. *Save them for posterity.* Purchase a news magazine that has a history-making event splashed across the cover and save it for your children or grandchildren. (You could do this with newspapers, too!)

OTHER PAPER GOODS

981. *Reuse sturdy disposables.* There are times when paper plates and cups are simply the most logical choice. We have discovered inexpensive plastic plates, however, which are a bit more sturdy for picnics and can be reused... without angst if a guest throws one or two away, since they are meant to be disposable. We have invested in these because we have shift after shift of company during summer months.

982. *We cut napkins in two* when just the family is eating. Don't laugh. And we never throw one away that hasn't been used. Grim thinks we're nuts.

983. *Use paper sparingly.* We rarely use paper napkins. We have a good supply of cloth napkins that do not need ironing. Napkins and tablecloths that require ironing are reserved for special hospitality.

984. *Use rags.* Paper towels are indispensable for some chores, but once you learn to use rags for cleaning you will never again reach for the roll. You will breeze by the paper towel aisle in the store and think smugly, "I used to use those things... before I became enlightened!"

Modern people, however, do not understand rag protocol. Dead socks and polyester-blended underwear do not make good rags. Neither do army tents, lampshades, silk stockings, or shower curtains. Good hard cotton, linen, terry, and muslin will take care of all your cleaning needs.

Alissa only buys paper towels when she has a puppy in the house. She figures she saves $30 a year on this item alone.

985. *Buy generic tissue and toilet paper.*

986. *Don't purchase purse-sized packets of tissue.* Buy it in big boxes (on sale, of course) and put a folded handful in a sandwich bag.

987. *Use two-ply toilet paper—it works better.*

988. *Cut down on over-use.* Problem with children using too much toilet paper? I read this in a magazine: Put the roll on the floor and step on it to make the roll "square." The paper won't spin as easily, so kids will know when to stop "rolling."

989. *Plain, old white generic two-ply is often less expensive.* I do not like dye in my septic or on my skin anyway.

990. *When buying tissue or toilet paper compare prices by checking to see how many "sheets" you get.*

DIAPERS

I used disposable diapers on Joshua. That was a long time ago. I was young and busy. Would I use disposables now? I probably would have them on hand, that's for sure! At the same time, I would remember the relative expense to me—and to the environment. Each year we dispose of eighteen million diapers in our country!

This book is about frugal living, about living within your means, about stewardship of belongings. But I have tried to keep it sensible; I wouldn't want to state categorically that you must use cloth on baby's bottom. You have to consider your circumstances and make the decision. However, even with time and utilities factored in, cloth diapers are much less expensive than disposable.

A friend was in the diaper business for a while. She told me about a study on diapers by the King County Nurses Association in Seattle, Washington. The following information includes some of their data, as well as some friendly advice:

991. *Think ahead.* When diapers are needed, they are needed NOW. Unless you have stocked your home well, the commandment on "knowing your prices" goes out the window! Price does not matter when baby is turning red with rage.

992. *How much are you spending on disposables?* Baby's diaper is changed between six thousand and ten thousand times before toilet training. If you pay $8 for thirty diapers and your child takes his time, you are spending a cool $2,666.64!

993. *Consider the longevity of cloth.* If you use cloth diapers you will have 100 percent cotton rags in the end. I know people who are still cleaning house with diapers from children born twenty years ago!

Diaper Cost Estimate for a Six-month-old Baby

Choices	Cost	Convenience
Washing your own	$5 - $9 /week (includes cost of diapers, soap, utilities)	Time and effort (Need pail, pins pants, or diaper covers)
Diaper Service	$9 - $13 /week (add cost of pins, diaper covers) Deodorized pail furnished.	Doorstep pick-up and delivery
Disposable	$10 - $13 /week (add cost of travel to store garbage)	No laundering, pins, covers (Must be disposed of)

994. *For a brochure on diapering practices,* send $1, along with legal-size self-addressed envelope to:

  King County Nurses Association
  9500 Roosevelt Way NE
  Seattle, WA 98115

SCHOOL SUPPLIES

I have fond memories of my new pencil case each year, of checking my "very important stuff": yellow pencils, fat erasers, rulers with geometric cut-outs, little scissors, pencil sharpener. I vividly remember sharpening pencils and reverently placing them back in the case. Do you have youngsters in school? Do you want to save money when you equip each this year?

995. *Buy colorful pencil boxes at a local discount store.* They will be on display when school starts, but buy these boxes *after* school has begun for next to nothing. Collect small items as the year goes on, for next year.

996. *Leslie puts together a box of tape, pencils, etc., and presents it to a preschooler as a birthday gift.*

997. *Buy highlighters, pencils, erasers, and tape at discount or bulk rate.* Visit an office supply store. Ask to see their monthly sale flier.

998. *Compare prices between local stores and an office supply catalog* (always consider postage and handling fees).

999. *Check the office or school supply aisle at the local warehouse store.*

1000. *For crafts and drawing at home:* Buy a large roll of butcher paper or check with the local newspaper and ask if they have excess newsprint that can be used for drawing at home. Local businesses have reams of computer paper that are perfectly clean on one side—all intended for the landfill.

1001. *Make your own memo pad.* Just about any once-used paper can be trimmed and banded together to make memo pads. We always have a creative assortment of notepads next to our phone.

Aftermath

And here you are at the end. But is it an end? Maybe not. This could be the start of your very own trek from the slippery money pit. It could be a happy reminder to roll up your sleeves. It could be incentive to dust yourself off and begin anew.

My wish for you is peace and joy as you inch along toward a frugal lifestyle. Contentment will come as you begin to live within your means: It is a bonus!

Let me end this book of hints with one last tip, one that you have read over and over in its pages, one that I give to you as encouragement. Let me take your hand and smile broadly as I announce to you with absolute certainty: You can do it! And have fun to boot!

SOLI DEO GLORIA.

Index